STAR GUITARS

Guitars and players
that have helped shape modern music

STAR GUITARS

Guitars and players
that have helped shape modern music

By Neville Marten

With notable contributions from
Rick Batey, Eddie Allen, Gibson Keddie,
Dan Eccleston, David Mead and Debbie Taylor.

MUSIC
MAKER
BOOKS

Music Maker Books Ltd,
Alexander House, Forehill, Ely, Cambs, CB7 4AF

First published in Great Britain in 1994 by Music Maker Books

Printed in the UK by The Lavenham Press, Suffolk

ISBN: 1 870951 15 8

Contents

FOREWORD
By Gary Moore

Outside the immediate world of the guitarist it's not often appreciated how much a player's choice of instrument can affect the music that he or she makes.

Few musical instruments are as expressive in the right hands as the electric guitar. Each guitarist plays with a different touch, a different feel and a different tone, and although it's become something of a cliche to say it, you really can recognise one note from BB King or one note from Jimi Hendrix. That's what separates one great musician from another and we should take care not to forget it.

However, there are other influences, over and above a person's abilities, which affect their sound; the permutations of guitar, amplifier and effects are endless, and even string and plectrum gauge can have a surprising impact on a guitarist. The basic fact, though, is that you don't play the same way on a Fender Stratocaster as you do on a Gibson Les Paul, because the guitars are made differently, they feel different, you respond differently to them and they react differently to you.

It was the tone of Eric Clapton's Gibson Les Paul on John Mayall's Blues Breakers album that turned me on to the sound of the electric guitar. But Eric's tone was very different from that of Jimi Hendrix, who of course was primarily a Stratocaster user. Peter Green, too, was a major influence. I was fortunate to tour with Peter when he was with Fleetwood Mac, and there can be no-one more sensitive in his choice of notes and tones. Towards the end of his time with Fleetwood Mac Peter sold me his 1959 Les Paul and it's a guitar I still use today because its sound and feel are unique.

Like most guitarists, including all those who influenced me - Clapton, Green, Jeff Beck, Jimi Hendrix and many others - I've used a variety of different instruments over the years, and today I choose whatever instrument suits my mood and that of the music I'm playing.

I hope this book gives at least some insight into the guitars and the players that have combined to make popular music as interesting and varied as it is today.

Gary Moore 1994

INTRODUCTION

Of all the elements that go to produce a musician's sound and style, one of the most influential is also one of the most overlooked: the make and model of instrument played.

Saxophonists, drummers, pianists and violinists will cite their Selmers, Ludwigs, Steinways and Stradivaris as proof of this, and go on to talk of supremacy of build, playability and tone. But no other musical instrument offers such broad tonal variety, character, personality and outright identity as the guitar; the electric guitar in particular. Aficionados might know the sound of a Selmer sax against, say, a Yamaha, and of course the tone of a Steinway Grand is legendary, but a Gibson compared to a Fender, or a Gretsch compared to a Rickenbacker, is like chalk, cheese, apples and oranges.

But there's a lot more to the choice of guitar than might at first seem obvious. For instance, what style of music will the instrument be called upon to produce? And what image does the player wish to portray?

In order to see why the guitar features so prominently in popular music we have to go back to the days of Rock and Roll. Prior to the mid fifties the guitar had been just another instrument: the lack of technology in relation to it had meant a continued background role; the guitar was rarely seen and even less commonly heard. And even when artists such as Charlie Christian and Eddie Lang showed what could be done with these new-fangled pickups and amplifiers, their influence - the quality of which cannot be overstated - carried on only to the next generation of jazz enthusiasts and jazz guitar-playing hopefuls, rather than captivating a wider market, which might have been expected.

So the instrument remained orchestra-bound, with no real identity of its own, and it wasn't until the emergence of Bill Haley, Elvis Presley and other American teen idols that the first quantum leap in interest occurred. And the odd thing is that these stars of the fifties probably had little idea that their arbitrary choice of instrument would have such a profound effect on the youth culture of their day. But it did, and when kids saw Haley's guitarist Danny Cedrone with his Gibson Les Paul, Presley with his Martin D-18 and The Ventures and Buddy Holly with their Fender Stratocasters, the die was cast.

Of course Rock and Roll was simple music - a few chords which any kid could quickly pick up and play - and the youngsters bought cheap guitars in their thousands to emulate their idols. Most of these instruments, whether from Sears or Woolworths, were probably discarded after only a few months and the real explosion had to wait until the early sixties, when those whose interest had not been just a temporary aberration, came of age.

Rock and Roll had been an American phenomenon, but the Beat Boom was British.

When the Brits sold Rock and Roll back to the Americans, repackaged and revitalised, the time was ripe for the kind of teenage rebellion that the electric guitar symbolised. Interest in the music was echoed by a fascination with the instruments that made it. In the UK, where American equipment had been largely unavailable, youngsters were fascinated by the names on the headstocks of their heroes' guitars - Rickenbacker, Gretsch, Gibson, Fender and Epiphone - and wanted to know more.

I was just into my teens when The Beatles' *Please Please Me* hit Number One in the British charts and, like a million others, was hooked. I watched the four moptops' every move, hung on to the lyrics of every song as though my life depended upon it. I wanted to **be** George Harrison. I studied his Gretsch Country Gent and his Rickenbacker 12-string and began to recognise the difference in their sounds. At school a few of us would huddle together and talk guitars - were Burns or Hofner actually the best guitars in the world, and could Harrison really outplay Marvin?

Like Gary Moore I was also one of the fortunate few who heard John Mayall's 'Blues Breakers with Eric Clapton' album when it came out in 1966. I was floored by the fire and verve in the young Clapton's playing and spent every waking hour trying to emulate him. Like Gary, it was the sound of that scorching Les Paul which did it, and because of it I was a confirmed Gibson fanatic for years. A little later, when Jimi Hendrix showed what a Stratocaster was capable of, my allegiance turned to Fender, but I was always mindful of the effect, both visual and sonic, that a player's use of a particular guitar could achieve.

My fascination with guitars was such that I studied the instrument inside and out. I became a professional guitar repairer, working for both Gibson's and Fender's UK operations and eventually wound up as Editor of *Guitarist* magazine, where I expressed my passion on a daily basis. But I can't forget my early days, nose pressed up against music shop windows, aching to own instruments like the ones I'd seen and heard my heroes playing.

Star Guitars hopes to appeal to anyone with an interest in the guitar, or in those stars who have used the guitar to say something in popular music. Limitations of space, however, have meant that there must be omissions; some musicians and manufacturers have been left out entirely, while others receive mention only in passing. In its choice of instruments and their players *Star Guitars* has tried to concentrate on the innovators, the leaders in guitar design rather than the followers, and the guitarists who have taken those instruments and used them to make a significant musical mark.

Neville Marten 1994

Acknowledgments

The quotes and many of the photographs used in this book have been taken from Guitarist reviews and interviews between 1984 and 1993. The author would like to thank all those whose contributions to the magazine have assisted in the compilation of Star Guitars. Many others helped in a variety of different ways. Please accept my apologies if, by some oversight, you have been omitted from this list:

Frank Allen, Richard Atherton, Tony Bacon, Carole Bates, Dr Christian Benker, John Birch, Graeme Bloomfield, Dee Bonham-Carter, Martyn Booth, Nick Bowcott, Rob Bradley, Chris Brennand, Robert Burns, James Burton, Penny Braybrooke, Dave Burrluck, Jeff Carpenter, Doug Chandler, John Coleman, Mike Cooper, James Coppock, Brendan Croker, Jamie Crompton, Ian Cruickshank, Paul Day, John Diggins, Lee Dickson, Dennis Drumm, Patrick Eggle, Trevor Elliot-Smith, Doug Ellis, Lizzie Ellis, Peter Else, Mike Emery, Alan Entwistle, Ron Eve, Neil Flemming, Martin Fredman, Linda Garson, Gordon Giltrap, Robbie Gladwell, Jack Golder (late), Mark Gooday, Alan Grant, Rob Green, Dave Gregory, John Hall, Phil Harris, Gavin Harrison, Rick Harrison, Pauline Heath, Bob Hewitt, Tony Hicks, Phil Hilborne, Dave Hill, Brian Hodgson, Adrian Hornbrook, Mark Noel Johnson, Adam Jones, Christine Keiffer, Peter Kent, Gerard Kelly, Mark Knopfler, Albert Lee, Michael Leonard, Graham Lilley, Alan Limbrick, Ivor Mairants, Peter Mant, Chas McDevitt, Charles Measures, Mitch Mitchell, Gary Moore, Barry Moorehouse, Gavin Mortimer, Roger Newell, Tom Nolan, Clive Norris, Steve Phillips, Marco Pirroni, Mark Prendergast, Suzi Quatro, Tony Sandeman, Andrew Selby, Jon Shrimpton, Linda Skewes, Mark Smith, Paul Reed Smith, Graeme Taylor, Phil Taylor, Chris Trigg, Len Tuckey, Jerry Uwins, Edward Van Halen, Guy Wallace, Marty Wilde, Bruce Welch, Hans-Peter Wilfer, Phil York, Tony Zemaitis

Chapter 1

Alembic

The coming of age of the bass guitar

The US Alembic company was among the very first to concentrate solely on the production of bass guitars. They grew in prominence from the mid-seventies onwards. Prior to this they had built both guitars and basses since 1969 and were - initially, at least - associated with The Grateful Dead, who used them in conjunction with their massive, self-designed P. A. system.

Alembic basses have always been expensive to buy, not only because of their individuality of manufacture, but also because of the guitars'

Alembic Series II Custom bass

unique design and sheer build quality. Alembic broke away from mainstream production principles by offering a selection of exotic body and neck woods, innovative onboard electronic tone systems and preamps, (including genuine stereo output which at that time meant playing through two separate amps). These departures, coupled with advanced design and assembly of the component parts, meant basses whose playability and potential tonal spectrum was hitherto unheard of.

Production of this type of bass coincided directly with a new breed of bass player. By the late seventies Jazz/rock and Funk music was placing great emphasis on technique and ability, and bassists in bands like Weather Report (Jaco Pastorius), Return To Forever (Stanley Clarke) and Chic (Bernard Edwards) were quick to lift the bass above its essentially supportive role, both rhythmically and harmonically.

Mark King with his Alembic bass

One of the first players to truly popularise the Alembic bass was Stanley Clarke, whose unique 'slap' style makes simultaneous use of bass and treble tones, with almost no mid frequencies at all. Clarke insists that his sound evolved as he changed to better and better instruments: "Early on, I was playing some really bad basses," he admits, "but trying hard to evolve to something that was good." Asked when he finally did find sonic nirvana, Stanley quickly replies: "I think it was the first time I got an Alembic bass..."

In the eighties, the new leader in this type of funky, rhythmic playing was Mark King of Level 42, whose main bass is still a wide-bodied Alembic. This instrument perfectly suits King's distinctive 'tucked-in' style, where his forearm lies along the strings, allowing him to spin his wrist, thereby slapping the strings against the top of the fretboard with his thumb. Mark, however, does not grow attached to any particular instrument... "I've been using Alembics since 1987, but I'm not very precious about the instrument. There are always fellows rushing up to say, 'Have a go with this,' and I plug it in

Allan Holdsworth's and James Taylor's bassist, Jimmy Johnson

and, maybe just because it's different, I think, 'Wow, that's great.' But I think it would be limiting to have the one instrument that was, like, your baby..."

Other notable Alembic users include ELP's Greg Lake, and John Entwistle of the Who, who commented: "I'd had all these 'Explorerbirds' made up, with Fender necks and (Gibson) Explorer bodies, but when I plugged an Alembic in, the difference in sound was ridiculous. We were rehearsing for a tour at the time, and with five days to go I rushed over to San Francisco and bought two more!"

Chapter 2

John Birch

Undisputed father of Glam Rock guitar

John Birch encapsulated the essence of the seventies with his daring and often bizarre guitars. The decade of Glam Rock saw bands like Slade, Mud and The Glitter Band taking to Birch's instruments as naturally as they did to their platform boots and outrageous stage getups.

Birch, who built guitars from his facility in Rubery, near Birmingham, did not set out as a builder of the

Above: Dave Hill's Super Yob
Right: Super Yob headstock

weird and wonderful, however. His initial aim was to improve upon the designs of, primarily, Gibson and Fender, who he believed were resting on fat laurels, neither giving the public what they wanted nor taking guitar technology further than it had come for thirty years.

So he and his team - which included John Diggins, now famous as builder of Jaydee guitars and basses, and a third team member, Arthur

Baker - set about designing better pickups and bridges for their guitars: pickups with additional pole pieces set in the gaps between the usual row of six, so that when a string was bent or slurred across the fretboard it remained in the pickup's magnetic field; bridges which were solid stainless steel and offered better adjustment than was currently available. Birch also poo-hooed some manufacturers' use of mahogany as a neck timber, saying that rock maple was a superior and far more stable material. More than this, he was one of the first of the modern makers - Rickenbacker had beaten everyone by decades - to utilise the neck-through-body design, whereby the neck extended through the entire length of the body, obviating neck joints of either the glued or screwed variety and creating a stronger assembly into the bargain.

Birch's regular guitars - often modelled around well-known and already popular styles - had beautifully slim necks and playing actions which seemed to defy the laws of physics, so low and easy were they to play.

But it was the guitars built for the big Glam bands of the day which made the Birch name famous in wider circles.

The 'Super Yob' was Dave Hill of Slade's trademark guitar. Actually designed by artist Steve Megson, the Super Yob was built by Birch and John Diggins. Dave Hill recalls that the design was originally devised purely to go with his outlandish outfits. It was supposed to represent a sci-fi raygun and was Hill's main stage guitar/prop from around '74 on, although Dave traded it in for two Gibsons

Mark King with a Jaydee bass, built by Birch's assistant John Diggins

asked the price and the guy said, 'You can't afford it.' So I asked again and he said, 'Five hundred quid.' I said, 'I'll have someone pick it up,' went straight out and said, 'Quick, go and find five hundred quid from somewhere!' And that's how I got it. They should have said five grand! Maybe I'd still have bought it. I'm a real Slade fan."

Although Dave Hill lost his love of the guitar a long time ago he's pleased about Marco's acquisition of it: "At least now it's being kept by someone who cares," he concludes.

As well as building instruments for most of the Glam bands of the day, John Birch also produced the distinctive left-handed guitars, shaped like Gibson's SG model, for Black Sabbath's Tony Iommi.

"The reason for that," states Iommi, "is that I couldn't get anyone interested in helping me. You wouldn't believe the amount of companies I contacted to try to get them to make me a guitar with a 24 fret neck! But then I found John Birch, who'd have a go at anything."

After some initial work on pickups for Iommi's guitars, Birch set about building for Tony what no-one else seemed capable of, or even interested in doing: the 24 fret guitar, where each string's length covers a whole two octaves.

"He really was the only one who would take a chance and build it," reiterates Iommi. "I've still got that guitar and of course now 24 fret necks are common."

John Diggins, one of Birch's original assistants, took over the building of guitars for Sabbath's riffmeister. These instruments were still very much in the John Birch style, Diggins using many of the original measurements and ideas and incorporating them into the new models. A feature which instantly distinguishes Diggins' guitars from those built by Birch is their unusual cleft headstock design. "It's based upon the two-fingered symbol of peace," explains Diggins, "and I eventually scaled it up to use on my Jaydee basses."

Tony Iommi, John Birch and John Diggins, it seems, were a trio full of ideas, many of which were years before their time, but which have become standard fare amongst today's guitar builders. As John Diggins resignedly points out: "Tony used to come up with some quite amazing ideas and we'd try and put them into practice. But we never seemed to get it beyond the initial idea before suddenly someone else would come out with it! It was very frustrating."

and a Fender at the turn of the decade.

"I felt that I'd outlived that period," admits Hill. "Slade were going through a rough patch towards the end of the seventies, slogging on the road and trying to survive, and I just decided I wanted to move into something else."

Dave Hill traded in the Super Yob to a Birmingham music store, who regularly hired the instrument out - the band Madness used it on a video for one of their songs - until eventually Marco Pirroni, guitarist with Adam and the Ants, saw it and offered to buy it. Pirroni takes up the story...

"We were playing in Birmingham and I was literally walking down the street when I saw the guitar hanging in the shop window. So I went in and

Chapter 3

Burns

The British Leo Fender?

If we are to talk in terms of British success and reputation in the pop music scene of the 1960s, no instrument company was more successful than that of Jim Burns, who began producing guitars under his own brand name at the decade's turn. Burns guitars were distinctive in appearance, the most instantly recognisable of them all being the Bison, with its exaggerated buffalo-style horns.

Although the popularity of Buddy Holly had created great interest in the Fender Stratocaster, no Strats made their way to British shores until Cliff Richard eventually ordered one for his guitarist, The Shadows' Hank Marvin. Whilst the band were pleased with the distinctive, not to say commercially successful sound of these guitars, the story goes that they were lamenting one day to Jim about the Strat's tuning inconsistency, when using the tremolo system. Burns, always an ideas man, promptly assured them that he could build a tremolo which would hold its pitch perfectly.

And so in 1964 was born the legendary Burns 'Marvin', of which only 350 were originally made and which did indeed utilise a more stable but bulky 'knife edge' tremolo - not found on other guitars with 'improved' tremolos until many years later. The Burns Marvin looked distinctly Strat-like in profile, and other features included a pseudo violin-style scrolled headstock, as suggested by Marvin, who used both white and distinctive 'green-burst' coloured versions. Another favourite of Hank's was his Double Six, a 12-string electric with an extremely long headstock - used most notably for the intro riff to Cliff Richard's hit, *On The Beach*. Prominent use of Burns guitars by The Shadows, coupled with a lack of available Stratocasters (and the subsequently hefty price tag should one appear), prompted other emerg-

Hank, with his Burns Marvin

ing British bands to opt for Burns guitars. Among a host of beat groups these included The Troggs and The Searchers, whose sound featured the use of the Double-Six especially. Even Elvis Presley was reputedly photographed with this model of Burns guitar.

Despite offering a varied range of well-made, well-designed guitars and basses - including the

Shergold Masquerader built by Burns sideman, Jack Golder

Burns Steer

monstrous Black Bison, a three-pickup, sycamore-bodied bass - and achieving a considerable reputation for quality and innovation, the fortunes of Burns receded as the sixties progressed. The company was bought out in 1965 by the American manufacturer Baldwin, with the instruments thereafter being referred to as Burns-Baldwins. After a continuing series of company reshuffles and relaunches, using original but ultimately unappealing body designs, the early eighties saw the Burns saga finally come to an end, The Shadows having long since reverted to playing Fenders.

Ironically, the Burns sound is still very much in existence. Queen's Brian May, who together with the help of his father, an oak mantelpiece, some motor cycle valve springs and a pedal cycle saddle-bag support, built his own guitar and chose to fit Burns Tri-Sonic pickups to it. These pickups have been heard on virtually every Queen recording, and so the sound, if not the guitars, of Jim Burns lives on.

To add further to the intrigue, Jack Golder - who was Burns' right-hand man throughout, and who formed Shergold Guitars during the mid-seventies - was, until his death in 1992, still building 'Marvin' models to order. Keeping these guitars as near original as was feasible, even using original parts where possible, Jack's order book was packed with orders from enthusiasts from all over the world.

Chapter 4

ESP

From spare parts to 6-string exotica

"I love my ESPs, they're just so well made and rugged," enthuses Metallica's guitarist Kirk Hammett. "I bang on them, drag them all over the place, throw them around. They built me a really cool-looking, black guitar with skull and crossbone inlays on the fretboard. It's one of my all-time favourites to play and I think I'll be having a lot more to do with that company."

Words of enthusiasm indeed. Kirk, and fellow Metallica axeman James Hetfield, both play guitars from the Japanese manufacturer ESP, one of many companies to have risen to prominence on the wave of eighties' Thrash and Heavy Metal.

Says Hetfield: "ESP always do exactly what I ask for and their guitars look and sound exactly how I

Batman comic guitar

Metallica's James Hetfield

want them to. They recently built me an *Of Wolf And Man* Explorer-style guitar with fret inlays showing a man turning into a wolf in stages. I was blown away when I saw what they'd managed to do".

One player to have had three models built and marketed by ESP is rock guitar supremo George Lynch, whose heavy and speedy technique is interspersed with tasty, bluesy notes. The three Lynch models are the Purple Sunburst Tiger Stripe, the Kamikaze and the Skulls and Snakes. All models feature only one control, a push-pull volume knob which doubles as a pickup selector.

"I hate guitars with countless switches and controls," says George, "but I also want the option

Kirk Hammett with his Flying Vee-shaped ESP

of a single coil pickup in the rhythm position - hence the push-pull function."

The ESP name first came to the fore with a range of high-quality replacement parts, including birdseye maple replicas of Fender necks and bodies, Gibson Les Paul and 335-style woodwork, as well as all kinds of pickups, scratchplates and hardware. But it's their custom-built instruments which have helped establish the company as a force in modern rock music: guitars like the custom-built Explorer-style instrument, which has been beautifully overlaid with a Batman comic - a technique perfected originally by covering a guitar in dollar bills! These guitars so highly reflect ESP's unique approach to guitar finishing (even though the instrument designs themselves are often less than original) that they are used to promote the company at Music Trade Shows around the globe.

Chapter 5

Fender

The unlikely genius who invented the Rock and Roll guitar

Leo Fender got things done. Unfettered by the preconceptions of a 'real' guitar maker, this unassuming radio repairman from Orange County, California changed the way guitars were made, and the way music was played. Fender, who didn't even play the instrument, turned the guitar into something that could be mass produced by relatively unskilled hands. Components which, by themselves, bore little resemblance to an actual musical instrument, were screwed together to produce some of the most formidable musical tools yet seen.

Telecaster

Look at the picture of this dismantled Telecaster and compare it to anything that had gone before. Gibson unflatteringly referred to the Tele as the 'plank guitar' and compared to their handcrafted archtops they weren't far wrong. A 1 3/4" thick slab of American ash for the body (often two or more pieces glued together) and a lump of Canadian

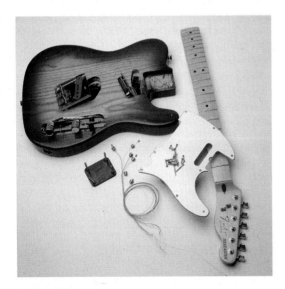

Exploded Telecaster

rock maple for the neck, a few simple electrics and the most basic of hardware was all it took to revolutionise an industry. The traditionalists may have scoffed, but once people realised that a solid electric guitar was a viable proposition, the craft of the luthier, as exemplified by Gibson, Epiphone, Guild, etc., must have seemed in jeopardy.

The Telecaster has been in continuous production, relatively unchanged, since 1950, and during that time the guitar has left its stamp on many great recordings. In fact, the Tele has

Keith Richards

probably as wide a range of advocates as any guitar ever made, the instrument being equally at home in Country, Rock, Pop, Jazz or Blues.

"It's still basically my favourite guitar," reveals Albert Lee, often touted as the world's finest country picker. "To me nothing feels like a Tele." Although rarely seen these days without his unusual Ernie Ball/Music Man guitar (see Music Man chapter) the Tele has always remained a constant friend. "My favourites are still the old ones," says Lee. "I have a '52 which I keep in London and a '53 which stays in the States."

Ex-Morrissey-Mullen guitarist, Jim Mullen, represents the opposite end of the Tele-player spectrum. Using just his thumb to extract the notes,

Mullen produces as 'jazzy' a tone from his Fender as does any archtop Gibsonite! "The Telecaster is really the only guitar I play on," insists Jim. "It's a nice simple guitar - one tone control and one volume control is as complicated as I want to get."

In the field of rock music the Tele has remained a stalwart. The Stones' Keith Richards removes the bottom E string, tunes the guitar to a chord of G and out comes *Brown Sugar* and *Honky Tonk Women*; Bruce Springsteen's use of the Telecaster highlights its role as the perfect electric rhythm guitar; and Jimmy Page is said to have used a Tele for much of his playing on the first Led Zeppelin albums - some of the heaviest Rock ever made. The Police's Andy Summers added echo and chorus effects to his Telecaster sound, played suspended and open chords and created the pop guitar sound of the seventies. "We were trying to create a wall, but a wall of space," says Summers, "using people's own

Tele master Danny Gatton

Late '60s Paisley Tele

minds to create the illusion of enormous sound."

Status Quo have been playing Telecasters for over a quarter of a century. Francis Rossi's famous faded green Tele (actually a refinish) and Rick Parfitt's white one have together bashed out more twelve-bar riffs than probably any other guitars. Using a wall of Vox or Marshall amps Quo take advantage of the Tele's rich but cutting tone;

Parfitt's rhythm playing is strong and incisive, while Rossi uses the Telecaster's powerful lead pickup, mounted on a modified bridge plate - "I could never understand why Fender used three screws to adjust the intonation on six strings," he explains - to create simple but distinctive solos.

The lads from Quo also use guitars from the late Leo Fender's last company, G&L Music Sales. As well as a blonde ASAT model Rossi had G&L build him a replica of his green Tele: "They took my guitar, which incidentally is supposed to be a '59, and when he got it he said, 'It's a '58' and I said, 'No, it's a '59' and he said, 'Sorry, I **made** it in '58!' So they made me this guitar and it's a copy of my green one, and it's one of the best guitars I've ever played."

Roy Buchanan was no household name, but he was a star to any guitarist who heard him. Roy used a clean, searing, sustaining tone to create an instantly recognisable Country Blues feel. Steve Cropper's Telecaster has been heard on hundreds of famous recordings. As the guitarist in Booker T And The MGs, the house band of Memphis-based Stax-Volt Records, Cropper backed such artists as

Above: Rosewood Tele, as used by George Harrison

Below: The greatly missed Roy Buchanan

Otis Redding, Eddie Floyd and Sam & Dave. Known for his choppy rhythm, interspersed with minimal lead licks, Cropper says of the Tele: "For a Booker T gig I wouldn't use anything other than a Telecaster. It's **the** sound. You just plug it in and go."

But the use of Fender's 'plank' in Rock and Roll goes right back to the fifties, in fact to Ricky Nelson and his teenage genius of a guitarist, James Burton. Burton went on to play for Elvis Presley and was the original guitarist in Emmylou Harris's Hot Band. He's still a top session player but it's his solos on the early Nelson singles on which his status as legend is founded. Burton more or less invented the modern art of string bending. By restringing his guitar - moving each string down a notch so the top E became the B, and the B became the G, etc., and filling the empty top E spot with a thinner banjo string - Burton provided himself with a slinky string set which begged to be bent and slurred. Asked why he chose the Telecaster he admits, "I just thought it was the neatest looking guitar in the shop!"

Although his most famous solos were played on his early fifties Telecaster, James is best known for his use of Fender's pink paisley version of 1968. "I had a call from the Vice President of Fender, who said, 'I have a guitar here that has your name on it,'" Burton recalls. "So I got in my car and went down to the factory. He opened the case and boy that guitar just jumped out at me"!

But how did his boss at the time, Elvis Presley, react to it? "I was playing *Johnny B. Goode* and

11

when it came to the solo Elvis came over and said, 'Play it James,' and I jumped in for the solo and the light caught the guitar and he did a double take. After the show he said, 'Man, where did you get that guitar? I love it! You've got to play it every night.'"

As well as the paisley, Fender have made several unusual versions of the Telecaster. George Harrison was presented with a solid rosewood Tele as a 25th birthday present from Fender. It was this guitar he used on the LP 'Let it Be' and on the roof of the Apple building in London to play such songs as *Get Back*, and *Don't Let Me Down*. Andy Summers' favourite Telecaster was his bound-edged sunburst Custom, into which a thicker-sounding and more powerful Gibson humbucker had been fitted in place of the guitar's original Fender neck pickup. The Thinline Tele - semi-solid and featuring a cello-style f-hole - has several committed users, incuding bluesman Lonnie Brooks and Simple Minds' guitarist Charlie Burchill.

Above: '50s trio of Tele, slab-bodied P-bass and sunburst Strat

Below: Quo's Rossi and Parfitt with their familiar green and white Teles

Stratocaster

The Telecaster was radical, broke all the boundaries, but Fender's next instrument was to set standards of design, playability, ergonomics and sheer desirability that the guitar makers of the world are still aching to emulate, let alone surpass.

Where the Telecaster had said 'function' and 'utility' the Strat screamed 'sex' and 'Rock and Roll'! The plankiness of the Tele gave way to the Strat's curvaceous lines, smooth edges, a body which gelled with that of the player (a local musician had suggested to Leo that the areas on the body where the forearm and ribcage rested could be carved away for comfort), and colour schemes which owed more to Chevvies and T-birds than to Guilds or Gibsons.

The first true Strat star was a bespectacled kid from Lubbock, Texas. Buddy Holly's picture, holding a sunburst Strat on the cover of the 'Chirping Crickets' album, enthused a whole generation of aspiring stars to take up the guitar. Also in America, The Ventures and The Treniers became keen Strat users. These bands were some of the first to take advantage of the instrument's great tremolo system, which not only provided greater pitch change but also returned the strings to near perfect tune.

Over in the far North of England a Buddy Holly lookalike was putting a Ventures-style band

Neo-classical Swedish whizz kid, Yngwie Malmsteen

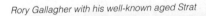

Rory Gallagher with his well-known aged Strat

The Shadows' Bruce Welch and Hank Marvin

together: The Drifters, soon to become The Shadows and British teen idol Cliff Richard's backing band. Marvin was a remarkable melody player; having marvelled at James Burton's work with Ricky Nelson, Hank decided he needed a Fender, although they were not available in the UK in the late fifties. Although he knew Burton was a Fender user, Hank made the mistake of assuming it must be the most expensive guitar in the catalogue, the Stratocaster, and it wasn't until after he'd taken possession of his Fiesta red Strat with gold plated parts, that he realised his error.

But Marvin quickly made the Stratocaster his own. "The Strat had a tremolo arm," recalls Hank,

Right: Buddy Guy

Below: Jeff Beck

"which I started to incorporate - there were no tremolo arms then, not in Britain anyway." The Marvin sound is clean and warm, but surprisingly Hank often favours the treble pickup, situated next to the bridge and normally associated with sharper, brighter tones. He explains: "If you hit the strings towards the bridge, the sound is harder, and more metallic. Towards the front, though, it's more mellow. If I'm using the tremolo arm, obviously I have to pick nearer the neck, so you get a rounder sound."

After Hank Marvin and The Shadows came the beat boom, and while Stratocasters were still abundant in these bands, the essence of the music demanded that they stay in the background. Lead lines tended to be played on Gretsches, with their nasal, twangy sound, or on 12-strings - Rickenbackers especially, although Tony Hicks of The Hollies preferred his Vox! Telecasters, too,

Above: 'The Shadows' album: Marvin, Welch and bassist Jet Harris all pictured here with Fenders

were favoured, for instance by Eric Clapton and Jeff Beck during their respective stints with The Yardbirds, as they exhibited a more incisive and meaty tone. Strats somehow seemed a little too weak and whimpish, and when the distortion and sustain capabilities of Gibson's Les Paul were discovered by the sixties Blues-boomers, the Strat was relegated to the role of rhythm guitar.

But then along came James Marshall Hendrix. Jimi Hendrix used a Strat like no-one had ever used any guitar. Jimi was left-handed, but played a right-handed Stratocaster upside down. Of course he had to swap the strings around too, which meant a fair bit of work, which Jimi liked to do himself. Hendrix's drummer and friend Mitch Mitchell explains: "Jimi would go into any guitar shop, anywhere in the world and get the stock Strat, take it back to the hotel room and spend a few hours setting it up. He knew exactly where he was with a right-hand, stock Strat, turned upside down."

Hendrix seemed to understand the mechanics of the Stratocaster: the way the pickups would feed back if the instrument was held at a certain angle to a loud amplifier (and Jimi liked his amps loud!); the way certain strings could be damped with the picking hand to prevent them feeding back, while simultaneously pulling out delicate melodies from the others; the fact that the Strat's tremolo arm could be used as an extra means of expression (as a reaction against the Hank Marvin school of playing the tremolo was 'out' by this time); the way that the Strat's three-way pickup selector could be lodged in between settings 1 and 2 and 3 and 4 to create two new tones.

Hendrix used all his knowledge and ability to extract every available sound from his Strat, and while he is famous for his use of distortion,

was not directly attributable to Hendrix was Irish rock and blues guitarist Rory Gallagher, whose initial fame came in the early seventies with his band Taste. Gallagher had picked up a rare Stratocaster, believed to be the first one in Ireland, back in the early sixties and today this same battered instrument, almost stripped of its original sunburst finish, is Rory's trademark. "I really like the Strat sound," says Gallagher. "It's good and clangy. I love the three pickups, I love the five-way selector and the way the volume and tones work. It's a tough guitar; you never have to treat it like a baby!"

Ritchie Blackmore, Deep Purple's classically-influenced lead guitarist, showed that a Strat could sound as fat as a Gibson and be played just as fast and just as furiously. But Fender's single coil pickups, notorious for picking up more than just the sound of the strings' vibrations, always proved a problem: "The guitar I use now actually has anti-buzz pickups in it. I used to have this tremendous buzz, to the point where the buzz would actually be louder than the notes I was playing. On stage I'd had to turn my guitar sort of upside down when it came to the solo, just so I wouldn't get this awful buzzing!"

Part of Blackmore's sound came from the fact that he 'scalloped' the fingerboards of his Strats by filing away the wood in the spaces between the frets. This assisted with both speed and vibrato techniques, as it allowed Ritchie to push the strings across the neck without his fingers dragging against the wood of the fingerboard. Swedish rock wizzard Yngwie Malmsteen followed Blackmore's example by scalloping his own necks, and listening to the two players you can hear a similarity in their feel -

Eric Clapton Signature Stratocaster

feedback and wah-wah effects, Jimi was a master of the tender, expressive note, and one of the finest exponents of blues guitar anywhere. Hendrix used the Stratocaster's wide tonal range better than almost anyone, before or since, and it was almost totally his influence which turned the Strat into the world's best selling, and most copied guitar.

One of the few players whose use of the Strat

heavy vibrato, a thick sound and lightning speed!

In modern blues the Strat has taken over from Gibson's Les Paul and ES300 series as the basic tool, although some players still choose the Telecaster, like 'The Iceman' Albert Collins, and Lonnie Brooks. Of course Gary Moore is a Les Paul man, B.B. King would not be seen without his 'Lucille' and the late great Albert King played a left-

The most famous Strat
player of them all, Jimi
Hendrix, who turned his
guitar upside down and the
Rock world on its head

handed custom Flying Vee. But almost everyone else, it seems, favours the Strat.

Although he made his name as a Blues player using mainly Gibson guitars, the unanimously elected Chairman of the Stratocaster-users Blues club is none other than Eric Clapton. Eric's switch from his Gibsons to the Strat seemed to coincide roughly with Hendrix's death - maybe he felt the guitar was too obviously Jimi's domain to use while he was alive - and his desire to play with purity and expression, as opposed to grit and fire. Eric's most famous Strat is 'Blackie', apparently a composite of several guitars bought in a Nashville music store in 1970 (the story goes that Eric purchased six and gave three away).

Dave Gilmour holding Stratocaster, serial number 0001

Blackie's V-profiled 1957 neck was E.C.'s favourite, but the guitar is no longer taken on the road. Clapton's guitar technician, Lee Dickson elaborates: "We had to have Blackie refretted, but with putting in the new frets, buffing up the edges and the fact that it had been stoned down once too much already, the E string was almost falling off the neck. So after twenty-odd years of use Blackie's gone the way of a lot of old guitars - happily retired."

Eric now uses a Fender 'Eric Clapton' Strat exclusively. The 'Clapton' was the first in a series of signature guitars from Fender and features an unlacquered, V-section neck, similar to Blackie's but with an extra fret and an onboard booster which allows Eric to dial in power and overdrive as he wants it. Other signature models include 'James Burton', 'Jerry Donahue' and 'Danny Gatton' Telecasters (Donahue is a country player whose multi-string bends, banjo-style picking and pedal steel-type effects make him a favourite of many guitarists. Gatton is similar, somewhat turbocharged and with a healthy slice of Jazz thrown in); 'Jeff Beck', 'Hank Marvin' and 'Yngwie Malmsteen' Strats.

Other Stratocaster Blues players include the sadly missed Stevie Ray Vaughan, whose quick-fire Texan style incorporated Country and Blues as well as the strong influences of Clapton and, most especially, Hendrix. "With Clapton, I learned how to make the sounds with my mouth, and then copied that with my guitar, kind of like scat singing," said Stevie. "With Hendrix's music I kept listening and kept trying and kept trying. Some of the things I just stumbled onto when I'd be playing, and things would kind of come to me..." Part of Vaughan's sound could be attributed to the fact that he tuned

Above: Ritchie Blackmore
Left: The influential 'Chirping Crickets' album featuring Buddy Holly's sunburst Strat

his guitars down a semitone, as did Hendrix, and set them up to be difficult to play. "I use the big necks, the V-necks," he said, "and jumbo bass frets. My action is pretty high too..."

Singer/songwriter/guitarist Robert Cray is another Strat-playing blues man. Cray prefers mostly clean sounds and uses his Stratocasters - his most famous being a silver-green '64 - to complement his singing and songs, rather than as an out-and-out lead player. Robert: "The Stratocaster has good highs and lows, a good clean sound. I find I can back up somebody with a nice chunky rhythm and if I want to cut through, it cuts like glass."

The Strat is also one of the best guitars for 'bottleneck' or slide playing. Ry Cooder's feel and touch with the slide is remarkable. Cooder sometimes plays a rare blue Strat with a rosewood fingerboard that's bound in white plastic. These bound necked guitars were a temporary aberration and only appeared for a very short time in the late sixties. Chris Rea, who admits to Cooder as his principal inspiration, plays fine slide guitar himself but, rather unusually, tunes his guitar to a chord of E major for both bottleneck and regular playing, lending added individuality to an already recognisable sound. Rea's favourite Strat, 'Pinky' named in deference to Clapton's 'Blackie', was bought because Chris believed Ry Cooder's blue Strat to be of the same

Fender convert, Eric Clapton and his Signature guitar

Gilmour fan, Toto's Steve Lukather playing a Strat style guitar built by California luthiers, Valley Arts Guitars

year: "I was still at that point where I thought, like most people who've just begun, that it's what you own as opposed to what you're playing." But Chris's Strat turned out to be just what he was

looking for. His guitar tech found the guitar and brought it to him: "The out of phase pickup setting was the most fantastic I'd ever heard. It's loud, and the tone is very wide, but it doesn't have the bite; it's very feathery."

Of all the Stratocaster users in rock music, no-one has a more recognisable sound than Pink Floyd's David Gilmour. Like most players, Gilmour has used a host of different guitars throughout his career, but David returns to the Strat as his favourite means of expression. Long, flowing notes, surrounded by tasteful effects characterise the Gilmour sound, making Floyd's guitarist one of his peers' best loved musicians. Steve Lukather, Toto's wizard guitarist says of David: "It's touch, and the way he presents his sound. You go and see Floyd live and you don't need to be on drugs; that's a drug in itself."

Gilmour possesses Stratocaster serial number 0001, a white model with gold plated parts. Although unlikely to be the first Strat ever made, this instrument is surely the collector's item of collector's items. Dave bought the guitar from his road manager Phil Taylor, who in turn had acquired it from pickup designer Seymour Duncan. "Seymour says he always meant it to come to me," reveals

Gilmour. "Eventually Phil wanted to borrow some money to buy a house, so I blackmailed him! I said the only way I'd lend him the money to buy the house was if he sold me the white Strat!"

The Fender Stratocaster has been cited as the world's most successful guitar. More instruments have been modelled after it than any other, and it's probably true to say that almost every modern guitarist has used the guitar at one time or another. After the death of Hendrix the use of the Strat as a serious rock guitar became common, with distortion - either from amplifiers turned up full, or from distortion-creating devices such as fuzz-boxes and overdrivers - ruling the roost. But then came a single called *Sultans Of Swing*.

Mark Knopfler did for the clean guitar sound what Clapton and Hendrix had done for distortion. Using no plectrum - just his thumb and two fingers - Knopfler coaxed pretty, country-style licks from his 1961 pink Strat, lodging the pickup selector (often

powerful as other guitars you can use a fantastic range of amplifier sizes. It's very flexible. You can play it like an acoustic guitar with a tiny little amplifier; these little old Fender amplifiers make Strats sound really really beautiful."

Although he made his name with the guitar's sound Knopfler hasn't used Fender Strats for years, preferring to play various 'hand-made' guitars.

Above: Larry Carlton and guitar by Valley Arts

Three of Mark Knopfler's guitars: a red Schecter, a maple Pensa-Suhr and a sunburst Custom Tele

taping it into position) between the neck and middle pickup positions to create what has become known as the 'Knopfler sound'. Of course Mark did not invent this sound, it was always there, but his fleshy touch, combined with his distinctive choice of notes, has made it his own. "I don't think there's much technique," says Knopfler. "I think I have got a sort of soul when I play, but I don't see it as being high technique." Of the Stratocaster he says: "Well, that thing between two pickups is an especially important aspect of the guitar, so you can get some kind of voice happening. And because it's not as

Companies like Schecter made their name putting together 'custom' instruments using exotic woods, pickups and hardware, but based very heavily on Fender's designs - Tom Anderson, for instance, who is currently one of the most highly-rated makers in the world, started up in business with Dave Schecter.

Knopfler has used several Schecters - primarily a red one, bound-edged and Tele-shaped - but more recently instruments by Pensa-Suhr. Pensa-Suhr guitars were originally built at the back of Rudy Pensa's New York music store by John Suhr. Suhr is not now associated with Pensa-Suhr, although at the time of writing the brand is still being assembled and hand finished at Rudy's.

Another manufacturer whose designs are strongly based on Fender models is Levinson of Switzerland. Gary Levinson is a clever guitar man who realised that the basics of good design were already there; in his eyes all they needed was a little improvement. So with his 'Blade' range Levinson added well-designed tone systems and tremolos, attractive finishes and very playable necks. Blade guitars and basses are highly regarded, and such artists as Chris Rea, Deacon Blue and Big Country are regularly seen playing them.

Jazzmaster and Jaguar

Conceived and marketed as the most expensive and luxurious Fenders of their day, the Jazzmaster and Jaguar have subsequently failed to secure for themselves quite the niche in guitar history that Leo Fender and sidekick Freddie Tavares originally foresaw.

Ironically, both models got off to flying starts (the Jazz in '57 and the Jag in '61). The slim, contoured and off-set body styling which the siblings shared certainly proved enticing to the player, and their common trem system (set back from the bridge and featuring a 'Trem-Lok' to aid tuning stability) found immediate favour among the twangy, warbling Surf guitarists. The Ventures' Nokie Edwards and Bob Bogle did great work toting Jazzmasters, and The Beach Boys' Al Jardine enshrined the shrill, tinkling tones of the shorter-necked Jaguar on such classics as *Fun Fun Fun* and *I Get Around*. It was a bright, good-time sound, and throughout the 'Surf Era' Fender's Jazzmaster and Jaguar

Blur's Graham Coxon with Jag

consistently outsold the 'workhorse' Strat and Tele, generally justifying their top-of-the-range designation.

So what went wrong? Basically, as Rock guitar playing exploded out of the Blues, the Jazz/Jag design began to seem increasingly inappropriate.

Bilinda Butcher, Kevin Shields' Jag-playing cohort in My Bloody Valentine

The shallow break angle of the strings over the bridge lent Fender's aristocrat a loose, rubbery feel, clearly unsuited to the violent attack and sustain of the new style. By comparison, the simple solidity of the Tele and Strat, unencumbered by the ingenious but fiddly tone controls of the Jazz and the even more intricate Jag, suddenly appeared that much more desirable. Significantly, only Magic Slim among the more prominent Blues players was ever known for playing a Jazz.

Neither is it a coincidence that the Jazzmaster had to wait for its rehabilitation until the advent of New Wave. In search of sounds untainted by what they saw as the clichés of seventies Rock and bored by the Blues tradition, late seventies guitar rebels recognised a natural ally in Fender's Jazz. New

York's Tom Verlaine adopted a sunburst model for Television's ground-breaking 'Marquee Moon' LP and wrung pure, glacial tones from the instrument. But, according to Verlaine, his choice of a Jazz was a purely financial one: "In the seventies, when guitars were still cheap, no-one wanted a Jazzmaster because they weren't loud and they didn't stay in tune. In '73, '74 you could buy a Jazzmaster for $150 easily. So that's why I started playing it. And then I got used to it, plus the vibrato arm on it is very nice. I use really heavy strings - like

Custom colour Jazzmasters flanking a custom colour Jaguar

a 0.14" to 0.58" - and that's another part of the sound. Live, I still use a Jazzmaster, always."

Others followed in Verlaine's influential wake. The Cure's Robert Smith set his introspective songs to the hollow, lonely sound of an Olympic White Jazz and still sports a version artily redecorated by a former girlfriend. Will Sergeant, a confirmed Verlaine acolyte, has used both Jazzes and Jags for the cutting, sixties-style tones of Echo & The Bunnymen. And proving that you can use a Jazz in anger, there's the raw crunch of Elvis Costello's early guitar work with The Attractions.

Though the thinner-sounding pickups and the shorter, 24 3/4" scale of the Jaguar have left it relatively more ghettoised, the fuller, more versatile sounds of the Jazzmaster have crowned it arguably the 'hippest' Post Punk guitar. More recently, it has become an 'Indie' staple, utilised by Kevin Shields for the ethereal drones of My Bloody Valentine, for the grungy rhythm and high-flying solos of J Mascis of Dinosaur Jr., for the avant-garde noise of Sonic Youth's Thurston Moore and by the Pixies' Black Francis because... well, because Francis likes The Ventures.

Blur's Graham Coxon is another Jag fan: "I've got a 1960s one which I really like, even though it

wasn't expensive. It gives off a really great dry sound and if you play it undistorted you get this cool cowboy sound, like that spaghetti western theme, *The Good, The Bad And The Ugly*. When you crank up the volume it does tend to slip out of tune quite a lot, though, which can be annoying. I think I bought it because J Mascis and My Bloody Valentine's Kevin Shields were into them."

And, as if the story of the Jazzmaster were not ironic enough already, nobody - but nobody - has ever played Jazz on a Jazz...

Fender basses

Although Leo Fender revolutionised the modern electric guitar he did not invent the instrument. What is to his complete credit was his inspired application of his principles to the construction of a completely new instrument: the electric bass, as it was originally called. Until the advent of the bass guitar, bassists in all musical styles had to rely on the double bass, an instrument beset with inherent problems. It was cumbersome, vulnerable and did not travel well; note-playing accuracy was questionable, even when the instrument could be heard behind newly amplified guitars. The Fender electric bass countered these problems; it was portable, it was robust, it was designed to be amplified and heard. Furthermore, guitarists-turned-bassists could play it!

The real bonus, however, was that it was a fretted instrument, allowing the bassist to play notes with 'precision'. And so 1951 witnessed the launch of the Fender Precision electric bass.

The original Precision closely resembled the Telecaster guitar with a 'slab' ash body, with the now familiar bolt-on rock-maple neck topped off by a Tele-type headstock. Like the Telecaster, everything about the new bass was straightforward.

Leland Sklar and his ancient autographed Precision

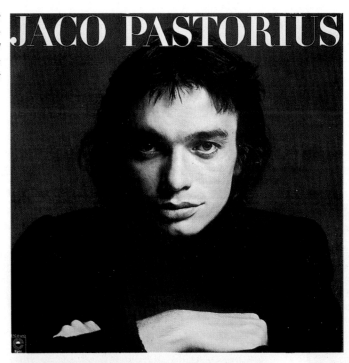

This, perhaps the most influential album of all time for bass players, showed Jaco Pastorius at his brilliant best

An early '60s Precision bass in Fiesta red

The styling of the Precision went up-market around the mid fifties when its shape began to echo the contours found on the newer Stratocaster. By 1957 the Precision looked very much as it does today. The instrument's original styling was reintroduced in 1968, in the form of the Telecaster bass, but this had little to commend itself over the long-established Precision and production of the T-bass model had ceased by 1980.

The launch in 1960 of the even more refined Jazz bass saw Fender finally win over remaining market resistance to the Precision. Overall, the Jazz (aimed at the more sophisticated 'Jazz' player) had a distinctly Stratocaster-ish look and possessed a slimmer and generally more manageable neck, as well as two pickups. These advanced specifications meant that the Jazz bass was not only less daunting to play, but rewarded the player with a broader tonal range than the more basic Precision.

Many definitive and inspired musicians have been associated with Fender basses. However, with the obvious exception of Paul McCartney (himself not a Fender user), The Shadows' Jet Harris and one or two others, bassists did not become featured players until the seventies onwards. Prior to this they were predominantly 'backing' musicians. In the previous decade this attitude was particularly applicable to two of today's most quoted bass influences. These players were members of 'house' backing bands: Motown's James Jamerson and Stax-Volt's Donald 'Duck' Dunn.

Whilst many people thrilled to the exciting and varied songs of The Supremes, Stevie Wonder, Marvin Gaye and other Motown artists, very few were aware that their funky, melodic and ever-inventive bass tracks were primarily the product of one man, James Jamerson, and his ubiquitous Precision bass. Likewise the R&B basslines of the great Stax recordings were all played by the MGs' Duck Dunn and his 1957, gold plated Fender Precision.

Dunn has stayed a Fender man throughout his career. "I've been faithful to Fender," insists Duck, "not so much them to me, though. I guess I've never been able to just call people and ask for something. Peavey have a good bass, called the Palaedium; it's got a great neck on it and it feels really good for slow songs, but I generally play too hard, so the Fender's the only one I can really attack. I tried a Hofner once and pulled the bridge off!"

Duck Dunn's main bass now is a hybrid Fender: a

Jazz neck on a Precision body. "The old Precision I've since put away," he admits. "Someone told me that Jaco Pastorius's Jazz bass went for about thirty-five thousand dollars in Japan, so I told my wife when I die to take my bass to Japan. I know I can't be compared to Jaco, but if there's collectors I say, 'Shit, don't bury me with it - sell it!'"

In the seventies, the Precision proved a worthy tool in the hands of such players as Deep Purple's Roger Glover, who remembers buying his first one with great affection: "I went home with it, stood it in the corner for about two hours loving every curve on it. When I got tired of that, I'd turn it round and look at the back for another two hours!" However, Glover's concerns were more than just aesthetic: "I really felt I'd 'made it' when I got my first Precision. Now I didn't have to worry so much about the sound; that had been taken care of. All I had to worry about was the playing of the bass!"

Bass-playing frontmen were well established by the mid to late seventies; Phil Lynott drove Thin Lizzy's brand of melodic Rock to great effect using a black Precision with his trademark 'mirror' scratchplate, whilst Sting made good use of a beaten-up Jazz in supporting the distinctive 'white-Reggae-Rock' sounds of The Police.

Duck Dunn mentions Jaco Pastorius and few could deny his importance and influence over modern bass-playing. Primarily known for his work with the Jazz-influenced music of Weather Report, Pastorius was a truly inventive player who made breathtaking use of chordal tones and swooping, counter-melodic structures. His well-used Jazz bass was converted into a home-made fretless by knocking out the frets, then using wood filler to plug the grooves!

The popularity of these instruments has never diminished. They continue to be viewed as robust and reliable workhorses, capable of adapting to any musical environment, surely a fitting tribute to the far-sightedness of Leo Fender. Bob Daisley, who has played with many of rock's leading musicians, including Ozzy Osbourne and Gary Moore, is an avid Fender Precision fan with a fine collection of both vintage Precisions and Jazzes. Bob still uses the first Precision he bought twenty years ago, but adds: "I'm not a vintage snob – I always buy them to play, because vintage instruments feel so inviting and the best ones feel as if they have songs in them."

Fleetwood Mac's John McVie has always used Fender Precisions: "I've been around the instrument circuit from A to Z, Alembic to Zon, and I always seem to come back to the P-bass. Unfortunately my original Precision got ripped off - that was a '62, I think - but my Fender now is comfortable for me, because it's the bass I started out with and I'm used to that neck width, which is like a tree trunk. A P-bass is very simple and sounds bloody good.

Once you've used one that's your yardstick for everything else."

With the advance in bass playing styles during the eighties came a parallel leap in instrument design, with both 5- and 6-stringed instruments being created to cater for the new bassists' ever-increasing technique. But Fender had done it two

One of the most recorded bass players of all time, Donald 'Duck' Dunn

decades previously. "I played a 6-string bass in '66 or '67," says Jack Bruce, Cream's classically trained bassist, "which I think are coming back into fashion," he adds.

Introduced in 1961, the Fender Bass VI resembled a low-strung guitar more than it did other Fender basses. Designed around the Jaguar/Jazzmaster body style the VI was tuned like a regular guitar but an octave lower, and its short scale length meant that there was no real depth to its tone. But you could play chords on it, as Jack Bruce demonstrated on Cream's 1967 single, *I Feel Free*. Other Fender 6-string players included The Hollies' Eric Haydock, who was seldom seen playing anything else.

Coming four years behind the Bass VI, Fender's Bass V was equally ahead of its time, but similarly failed to enthuse the bass players of the period. Modern fives have the extra string on the bottom, tuned to a B below

Jimi Hendrix's bassist in The Experience, Noel Redding

the normal bottom E. But Fender added their fifth at the top - a C above the usual G. This did provide the bassist with much increased flexibility, as he could move across to the next string rather than sliding up five frets, the musical equivalent. But while the Bass V was probably a more worthy instrument than the company's 6-string bass, it was actually discontinued five years earlier, in 1970.

In the company of such successes as the Telecaster and Stratocaster, Precision and Jazz bass, Fender's 6- and 5-string basses may seem like failures. But in terms of the evolution of the electric guitar they illustrate just how advanced Fender were in their thinking, and just how important to the development of popular music this one company proved to be.

Fender's futuristic but unappreciated Bass V

Chapter 6

Front men and women

David Bowie looking good with a Gibson Country Gentleman guitar

Guitars as fashion statements or musical instruments?

One major role the guitar is often called upon to perform is that of stage prop. Invariably the instrument hangs around the artiste's neck in the playing position, or dangles headfirst towards the floor, adding extra visual impact to a performance while at the same time helping to reinforce the desired image of 'musician'.

Many stars are as well-known for their performance *with* a guitar as on it, although of course many are more proficient on the instrument than we might give credit for.

There are relatively few frontmen or women who

fall into the category of total poseur - they can nearly all play *something*! Elvis Presley, for instance, was a pretty good strummer, with a great sense of rhythm, although watching his early films it appears that whatever guitar he was using - most commonly Gibson or Martin acoustics - he was capable of playing the song, kissing the girl and driving the car at the same time.

Queen's late singer, Freddie Mercury, was a fine pianist and also a reasonable guitarist, and he could often be seen strutting his white Fender Telecaster on stage, reinforcing Brian May's rhythm work or underpinning his solos. Live, U2's Bono likes to strum, among other things, a Washburn electro-acoustic, adding percussive texture and shimmer to the band's moodier numbers. Another player in this category is David Bowie, who uses a wide variety of guitars on stage but definitely chooses the instrument to go with the occasion.

Of course Bowie writes great songs on the guitar so he obviously has a good understanding of chords, etc. Likewise, Elvis Costello's use of the Fender Jaguar is not confined to that of the image provider - although it created enough of one to help spark off a Jaguar/Jazzmaster revolution! British fifties Rocker turned Christian megastar, Cliff Richard, is a most competent fingerstyle guitarist, having played Aria guitars for a long time. Of

Singer, songwriter, multi-instrumentalist and huge talent, Prince

Above: Freddie Mercury strumming an Ovation
electro-acoustic

course, like any other frontman/musician Cliff will choose different guitars, either electric or acoustic, as and when the fancy takes him.

Chrissie Hynde's blue Telecaster provides a necessary chordal element in The Pretenders' music, and other female artists like Joni Mitchell and Nanci Griffith would be rightly insulted if their musicianship was seen as secondary to their singing and songwriting.

The Pretenders'
Chrissie Hynde with
her trademark blue
Telecaster

King of the frontmen: Elvis
Presley with a customised
Gibson Dove

Bruce Springsteen and Bryan Adams both supplement their raspy vocals with heavy chords and riffs - again, having generally used their guitars to compose the songs in the first instance.

Certain stars have tended to hide their guitar playing prowess behind their frontman exteriors. For instance, Prince's abilities as singer, songwriter and producer are legendary, but this world class lead guitarist chooses his moment to shine on the instrument. Likewise, Marc Bolan's abilities as a lead player were quite acceptable, but he relegated his playing to a secondary rhythm role on most of

his hit chart successes, although *Ride A White Swan* features a fine solo from Marc.

So it would seem the majority of frontpeople have at least a certain amount of guitar-playing ability - even the greatest frontman of them all, Mick Jagger could hold his head up as a strummer. But one thing's for sure, for the best pictures, the most memorable media moments or for that most credible musicianly look, no frontman or woman should be seen without a guitar somewhere about their person.

Chapter 7

Gibson

The standard by which all others are judged

Tradition and craftsmanship are the hallmarks of the American guitar company Gibson. Their guitars may not be futuristic in the same way as Fender were in the fifties or Steinberger in the eighties, but the sound of Gibson instruments has coloured popular music for a century.

It all started back in the late nineteenth century with a guitar player from Michigan called Orville Gibson, who made remarkable instruments in his spare time. The Gibson company proper was formed in 1903 and they soon grew to dominate the market in mandolins, mandolas and harp-guitars (and after the war they did equally well in the banjo boom too). But their best move came in 1920 when they employed Lloyd Loar, who not only set the standards in mandolins and banjos but single-handedly invented the acoustic f-hole guitar.

Throughout the thirties, forties and fifties Gibson had virtually every well-known jazz guitarist endorsing their products. However, although they mounted pickups on their standard guitars from the late thirties onwards, they were slow to react to advances in technology; in fact, these arch-traditionalists regarded the appearance of the solid electric guitar with absolute horror!

Les Paul

At this point another brilliant inventor and designer enters the picture. Les Paul, who pioneered the multi-tracking without which modern recording methods simply would not exist, was also an early experimenter with electric guitars, and he built a guitar nicknamed 'The Log' from old Epiphone parts, but with a solid centre-section. In his own words:

"I was in Chicago with The Log in 1941, saying, 'Here's the way you should be going, Gibson.' And Gibson were going, 'That weirdo's in town again, the one with the broomstick with the pickup on it - duck him!' And then Leo Fender came along with his guitars and immediately I got a call from Gibson saying that they wanted to put out my guitar. The contract they sent out was beautiful - I'm going to frame it! There was a clause that said that they might not even want to use the name Gibson, and

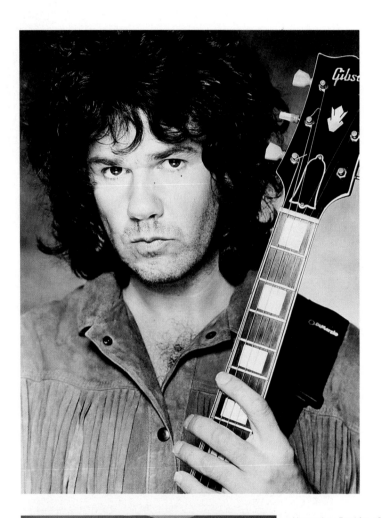

Above: Les Paul fan, Gary Moore

Left: Early '50s Les Paul goldtop

the President asked me for suggestions for what to call the guitar. I said, 'Why don't you call it the Les Paul guitar?' He said, 'Will you put that in writing?'

"And that's how the Les Paul was born. If it hadn't been for Leo I'd never have got that call, and I thank him for rattling Gibson's cage!"

Les Pauls are now considered some of the all-time classic rock guitars. With their mahogany and maple construction and proper glued-in necks they're almost like scaled-down jazz guitars. And they generally sound much fatter and warmer and exhibit a far longer sustain than spikey, thin-sounding Fenders. Gibson wanted to differentiate themselves from Fender so they decided to carve an arch into the front of the new model because they knew that Fender lacked the

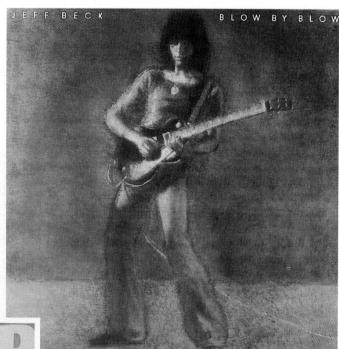

Jeff Beck's seminal album 'Blow By Blow', on which he used, among other guitars, this nearly black Les Paul

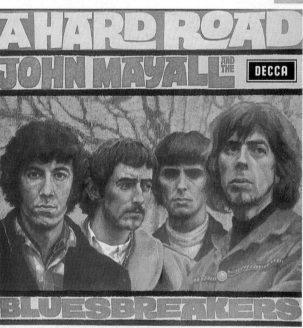

John Mayall's 'A Hard Road', on which the great Blues guitarist Peter Green first came to prominence

machinery to do the same. The earliest 1952 Les Pauls were painted gold and had cream-coloured single-coil pickups; by 1957 the famous double-coil humbucking pickups had appeared, designed by Gibson employee Seth Lover (one pickup was wired out of phase with the other, therefore cancelling, or 'bucking' the hum that single coils were renowned for) and a year later in 1958 they introduced the fabulous 'sunburst' flamed maple top. (This use of fine-grained timbers was another thing separating Gibsons, Epiphones, Guilds and so on from Fender guitars, which were built from fairly ordinary ash or alder.)

Strangely enough, the Les Paul was not initially very successful - Gibson ceased production in 1960 - and it took an entirely new breed of player to discover that the Les Paul's weight and sustain worked superbly in conjunction with the inefficient but musically distortable amplifiers of the mid-sixties - a sound that became the root of the 'Blues boom'.

Michael Bloomfield, with his group The Electric Flag, was a massive early Blues/rock influence. Initially he was playing a '52 Telecaster and when the prices of these guitars shot up overnight he discovered 'goldtop' Les Pauls, but finally settled on the sunburst instrument that would become his trademark. Suddenly, the Les Paul was in fashion. Eric Clapton used a Les Paul with John Mayall's Blues Breakers, as did his successor in the band, Peter Green (later of Fleetwood Mac) and *his* successor, Mick Taylor (later with The Stones). Clapton primarily favoured the pickup at the bridge for his sharp and fiery sound, but discovered that by selecting the neck pickup and backing off the tone control, a thick and flutey sound could be created. When Clapton used this sound in Cream - not only with Les Pauls but other Gibsons, like his cherry red ES335 and the famous psychedelic SG Standard - the sound was christened 'woman tone', due to its soft and feminine qualities. Green's Les Paul tone was equally distinctive; using less distortion than Clapton, but often drenching his guitar sound in reverb, Green was the master of the haunting blues. But there was another secret to his sound. While his guitar was being serviced, the repairer accidentally fitted one of the pickups' magnets the wrong way round, so that when the centre position on the selector switch was engaged (both pickups on), the pickups were out of phase with one another. Green liked the sound so much that he kept the guitar this way, and recorded some of his most famous and distinctive works using this

Above: The Cult's Billy Duffy with a natural finish Les Paul Custom
Below: A 1958 Les Paul Standard owned briefly by Gary Moore

tone - Floctwood Mac's *Need Your Love So Bad* and *Stop Messin' Around* are particularly good examples.

For many years the top of the range Les Paul, the ebony Custom

Throughout his career Jeff Beck has used a Les Paul to enormous effect, often switching pickups and altering the guitar's tone and volume settings mid-song. Beck is one of those rare players whose technique can override the instrument that he's playing, so that a Gibson can be made to sound like a Fender and vice versa. This is especially evident on his seventies solo albums, 'Blow By Blow' and 'Wired'.

Jimmy Page carried the Les Paul fully into the seventies with Led Zeppelin, as did the much-missed Duane Allman with The Allman Brothers; since then the torch has been carried by other stars like ZZ Top's Billy Gibbons (who calls his favourite 'Pearly Gates') and the late Randy Rhoads with Ozzy Osbourne, who favoured a cream coloured 'Custom' model.

Sunburst Les Pauls from 1958 to 1960 are still the most sought-after solid electric guitars in the world; prime examples on sale these days can command outrageous prices. In fact, in Japan a pristine example made a staggering $100,000!

Gary Moore is one player who actually *uses* these fine old guitars, instead of locking them away in bank vaults. He's got a '57 goldtop and two '59 sunbursts - one of which is Peter Green's guitar, still with one humbucker wired 'out of phase'. "I think that if you have these guitars then you should play them," says Gary. "That's why I don't buy mint ones - they're all beaten up, so you can take them on the road. All mine are very different to play, and the Peter Green one's the hardest of all. It's got a very stiff, high action and most people would find it a nightmare to play because it's got such a big neck."

For those of us who can't even afford beaten-up '59 Les Pauls, Gibson started making the model again in the late sixties and they're still one of the raunchiest guitars around. "I think you have to go a long way to beat 'em," says Motorhead's Phil Campbell. "You can play Jazz on them, or Blues, or heavy Rock - just about anything. They're not the ultimate all-round guitar, but you'll never get a Strat to sound as ballsy as a Les Paul."

Def Leppard's late lamented guitarist Steve Clarke revealed a secret: "When I was a kid, I used to go into guitar shops and actually get off by touching a Gibson Les Paul! It might sound weird, but that's the way it was. I use a Les Paul because of Jimmy Page - us Page freaks always wear Les Pauls hanging at about knee height!"

Ozzy Osbourne's recent guitar-toting whizz-kid Zakk Wylde agrees. "Les Pauls rule!" he declares. "Those suckers have balls. Once I'd got my first one I just had to have more, and I saved every penny I made from giving guitar lessons so I could get another!" And the early 'goldtop' Les Pauls have their devotees too, like John Martyn, whose use of special tunings and washes of ethereal effects create a most distinctive sound: "My '54 Les Paul is my favourite guitar of all. It's so sweet to play, and you can get any noise out of it you like. The old P-90 pickups do buzz a bit, but they're just so powerful that it's insane!"

Although The Cult's Billy Duffy is a Gretsch man, he uses Gibsons as well. "All my Les Pauls are seventies Customs and I put Seymour Duncan 'Jeff Beck' pickups in all of them, because they're a bit thicker in the mid-range. Les Pauls do tend to blend

Guns N'Roses' bad boy guitarist, Slash, who aided the '80s/'90s revival of the Les Paul

together when you get as many firing on a record as I do!"

In recent years, Guns N'Roses guitarist Slash's almost exclusive use of Les Pauls has given the old warrior yet another boost. But Slash is modest about his influence: "Gibson's going, 'Well, you just brought the Les Paul back' and I'm, like... 'What?!' I mean, it's a certain kind of sound that you can only get from a Les Paul, and I realise that the whole flash, speed guitar style that Eddie Van Halen brought around really messed Gibson up, business-wise. But that's no reason for me to believe I brought the Les Paul back. The Les Paul was always there, it's just that no-one was using them."

Slash favours vintage Les Pauls in the studio, but his main stage guitar is one which Gibson built him specially: "Gibson build me guitars all the time," he enthuses, "but they've only come up with so many that are actually usable; the other ones I send back. I've got one Les Paul Standard that's my main guitar and I've had that ever since I signed my deal with Gibson - they haven't been able to duplicate it. I have one that's like a B version of that, and I've got a goldtop which I also use. I recently got a black Standard which they never lacquered, so it's completely matt black, it's really great looking and on the back it's got, 'Hold this for Slash' etched in it. I got it before it was finished and I said, 'It's great, leave it.'"

A Les Paul 'TV' Junior, so named because the limed mahogany finish showed up well on television

So the guitar which Les Paul designed has been around since before Rock began and looks unlikely to roll over and die for a long time to come.

The SG

Gibson's SG (Solid Guitar) has been the chosen tool of players from AC/DC's Angus Young to Frank Zappa. Angus: "The guitar I always looked at, if I

A pair of SG Specials, both with retro-fitted humbucking pickups

SG Standard in Cherry

got a catalogue, was an SG, and I was probably the only one that went, 'I want *that*.' So the first chance I got, when I got some money, I bought one. And the one I bought I still have now. Its head has been broken and it's been trodden on... but I always get it fixed."

Angus has never been able to replicate his original SG: "After 'Highway To Hell', which was when I first had some money, I said to myself, 'Right, now I'm going to try and find a couple of SGs like my original one.' But it's funny, I've never sound one the same."

Black Sabbath's left-handed guitarist Tony Iommi is known for using an 'SG' which was in fact a custom guitar by English maker John Birch. Subsequent instruments were made by Birch's successor, John Diggins, although Iommi is now back using Gibsons. "I've tried all sorts of guitars," shrugs Tony, but for some reason I've always come back to SGs."

Tony's early move away from Gibsons was due to him simply 'going off them', although one incident may have been the catalyst: "What really rubbed salt in the wound was they sent me three new guitars and they were all *right-handed*!"

Gibson designed the SG to take over from the floundering Les Paul in 1960, but Les Paul didn't approve. "The first one I saw was in a music store," he says, "and it had my name on it, but I didn't like the shape - a guy could kill himself on those sharp horns! And it was too thin, the neck was too skinny, and I didn't like the way the neck joined the body. So I called Gibson and told them to take my name off the thing."

Indeed, many SG users seem to enjoy a love-hate relationship with their guitars. "I stopped playing the SG," says Carlos Santana, now a PRS user, "because mine just wouldn't stay in tune - the neck kind of flapped around all the time!" Pete

Townshend would agree: "I never had any problem in smashing SGs," he says. "They were just like balsa wood." Actually, Townshend does have a heart: "The only guitar I ever really cared about was my Gibson J-200 acoustic," he continues, "and one day it got wet in the studio and just sort of exploded - perhaps it was the guitar getting back at me."

Flying Vee

Many other Gibson guitars have places in Rock's hall of fame - like the famous arrow-shaped 'Flying Vee', beloved of Blues players and Metal guitarists alike, from Albert King through to Michael and Rudi Schenker, as well as some pop players, like Dave Davies of The Kinks. The main thing about Flying Vees is that they're murder to play sitting down, and yet they do sound fantastic.

Although Jimi Hendrix played various Gibsons on record - he particularly liked Les Pauls for Blues - a custom-built Flying Vee was the only Gibson guitar that Jimi used with any regularity. Maybe it was for the same reasons as Wishbone Ash's Andy Powell: "I chose the Vee for the sound; they're very sharp, they really cut through, but there's a real richness to the early ones. Mine's a '58 - it balances really well,

Andy Powell surrounded by his Flying Vees

Rudi Schenker with his familiar two-tone Flying Vee

the action is excellent and the neck is a little wider and deeper than the mid-sixties ones I have."

Explorer

Similar to the Flying Vee is the radically-shaped Explorer, introduced in the late fifties to little or no response but now boasting a list of famous users from Eric Clapton to U2's The Edge. "It's only good for certain songs," Edge admits, "and although it's not as versatile as a Strat, it does do one thing very well."

300 Series

As well as his Fenders and his Explorer U2's Edge also plays one of Gibson's most consistently cherished models, the semi-solid ES335. "I've got an old '58 ES335," he proudly states, "which is interesting because it's got the attack of a Telecaster and the depth of a Les Paul."

Edge is dead right about the 335, a slimline semi with two equally-sized rounded cutaways. They were one of the first electric guitars designed to do everything really well, and they're still classics. It's impossible to imagine Chuck Berry with anything else, although he commonly used a variety of Gibsons. Blues greats like Freddie King and Otis Rush have all used variations on the 335, and B.B. King will always be associated with Lucille, his Gibson ES355 which has now been modified under the direction of King and is actually marketed as the Gibson 'Lucille' model. White Rock and Blues artists have followed suit - Clapton in his Cream days and Ten Years After guitarist Alvin Lee, whose bright red, sticker-covered 335 is virtually a Rock landmark: "I bought mine in Nottingham," Alvin reveals, "for £45 - that has to be the best investment I ever made! The reason it's still covered with the old stickers is because I once snapped the head off and when it came back from being repaired, they'd lacquered over the stickers! It's still my main guitar and I love 335s - Les Pauls always feel too small and heavy for me."

B. B. King and his Custom ES355 'Lucille'

Above: Variants of the 300 series, left to right: ES330, ES345, EB2 Bass, ES335, ES355

Below: Alvin Lee and his sticker covered ES335

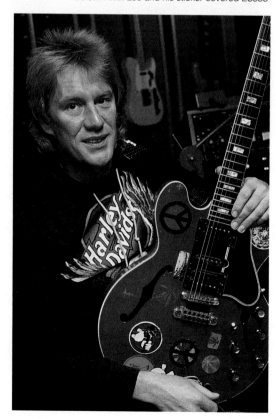

However, many guitarists have now stopped using 335s in favour of Fenders or Fender-derived guitars. Larry Carlton, who played with The Crusaders, Steely Dan, Christopher Cross and dozens of others, was actually nicknamed 'Mr 335' and named his studio 'Room 335', but now plays a Valley Arts Telecaster-style guitar. However, Carlton had been using, and praising, Mike Maguire's small Californian repair and customising company for years: "Mike Maguire made a customised 'Strat' for me, for the 'Sleepwalk' album. But I couldn't play a Strat because of the angle of the tailpiece compared to the 335 - I couldn't pick fast on it at all. So I started dabbling in solidbody guitars." Asked about his current Valley Arts he says: "Really it's a hot-rodded Tele. It's closer to a Tele style than a Strat, but it's so completely different..."

Session maestro Lee Ritenour, another Valley Arts convert, says, "I haven't used a 335 since about 1982 - with the humbucking pickups it just doesn't cut through the contemporary sounds that well."

An interesting point about the sound of the various Gibson models is that generally speaking they feature very similar pickups and control systems, and therefore it is the construction methods of one guitar compared to another which determines their different sounds. Take a Les Paul

Above: J180 'Everly Brothers' Jumbo

Who's John Entwistle, among others. Roger Glover of Deep Purple tells a strange tale about his Gibson Thunderbird bass: "I was playing with Rainbow, and we'd just reached the last chord of the very last song, when suddenly I couldn't feel the strings. I looked down and the whole head had disappeared! T-birds were very weak at that point. I must just have touched the mike stand and - whack! - instant headless bass!"

Others..

Perhaps the most remarkable thing about Gibson is that they make so many different kinds of guitars so well. In addition to straightforward Rock guitars like the Les Paul, Flying Vee and SG, they build superb jazz guitars, monstrous twin-necked electrics - favourites of seventies stars like Jimmy Page, Steve Howe and John McLaughlin - and a whole range of excellent acoustics, used by everyone from Elvis Presley and the Everly Brothers (the J-180 was known as the 'Everly Brothers' model) to The Beatles, and thousands of others. Gibson electric guitars might not be considered as adaptable as Fenders but they've been used by everyone from Bob Marley to the Sex Pistols, and for some musicians they're still the only 'real' guitar.

Standard, an SG Standard and an ES335 for example. They share more or less identical pickups and electrics, and yet the Les Paul, with its solid mahogany body with thick maple-slabbed top is powerful, middley and sustaining, making it ideal for Rock and Blues; the slim but solid-bodied SG is sharper, but still warm-sounding, making it a good heavy riff guitar; and the semi-solid ES335 is warmer still, and smoother, yet brighter at the top, making it more sensitive to the dynamics of picking and suiting it to almost any style of playing.

Gibson basses

Gibsons have never had the treble output of Fenders, so they often have trouble in competing with the strong midrange sound of the modern synthesiser. And for exactly the same reason - their warm sound - Gibson basses have never achieved mass popularity, although they've been used by Cream's Jack Bruce, Free's Andy Fraser and The

Gibson and Epiphone

In the early fifties the highly respected Epiphone company closed its doors for the last time and many of its employees went to work for Guild. In 1957 Gibson took control of Epiphone lock, stock and barrel and throughout most of the sixties Epiphones were made alongside Gibsons in the Kalamazoo factory, often sharing bodies, electrics and hardware, but always retaining the distinctive Epiphone headstock. The most famous Epiphone users were The Beatles' John Lennon and George Harrison, who both owned Casinos - ES330-style semi-acoustic guitars. Lennon stripped his tobacco sunburst instrument bare of finish and in photographs this looks like a regular blonde Casino. Other Epi players were the lamented Steve Marriott who often used a solid-bodied Crestwood in his days with Boogie band Humble Pie.

Of course, the popularity of Gibson guitars ensured that other manufacturers would want to get in on

The Gibson-made Epiphone Casino

the action, and cheap copies of the best makes have always been rife. But during the late sixties and early seventies Gibson encountered a problem with quality, as did Fender, due the the sheer volume of demand for their products. So certain limited-output makers stepped into the breach and began making 'up-market' versions of Gibson models.

Hamer was one such manufacturer and probably Hamer's best-known guitars are their early maple-topped versions of the double cutaway Les Paul Junior and an equally stunning, bound-bodied Explorer. Although these were used by such bands as Cheap Trick, whose guitarist Rick Nielson was often seen with multi-necked, multi-coloured versions, and artists such as Gary Moore, Hamer now concentrate on building guitars which, while original in design, owe as much to the Fender camp as to Gibson's designs.

High quality Hamer guitars, very much in the Gibson Les Paul Special style

Chapter 8

Gretsch

Rockabilly Rebel meets Country Cousin

The Gretsch guitar is a mass of contradictions. At some points in Rock history they've been the coolest things with six strings, while at other times no self-respecting musician would have been seen dead with one! They're not nearly as robust and well-made as Gibsons, but some of them still fetch huge prices on the collector's market. They're possibly the ultimate Rock and Roll guitars, but whereas Fenders are sleek, streamlined and futuristic, Gretsches are a weird mixture of the traditional and the gimmicky. They're ungainly, usually awkward to play and often covered with gadgets and trickery like sparkle finishes, tremolo arms which don't do much, cushions to protect the paintwork, string mutes, stereo pickups and devices designed to modernise their old-fashioned, plunky sound. But they're still basically cowboy jazz guitars.

All the same, Gretsches have an extensive fan club. Eurythmic Dave Stewart is a big Gretsch freak, often using a Country Gent or the company's

The 6120 Chet Atkins: Gretsch's most renowned model

Early '50s G-brand Round Up, model 6130

top-of-the-line, gold-plated White Falcon guitar, and here's how he sums up their quirky appeal: "Gretsches? They're just so cool! The main trouble with them is that it's really hard to get them to sound right, but when you do they're raunchy, but sort of woody and mellow at the same time. The thing is that they're like old cars in a way - you use them differently to a modern guitar."

Old cars is a very good comparison. The Gretsch company dates right back to 1883; initially they made tambourines, but then moved on to banjos and drums before starting serious production of Jazz-style guitars in the early thirties. But just like American cars, most 'classic' Gretsches come from the fifties, which is when the company called in possibly the best-known player at the time, the Country Swing guitarist, Chet Atkins.

"Gretsch used to come to me all the time, wanting me to play their guitars," recalls Chet. "I was happy playing my handmade D'Angelico at the

This Double Anniversary is in two-tone Smoke green

time, but they kept on at me and so I said, 'Well, why don't you let me design you a guitar the way I want?'

"The outcome of that was the Gretsch 6120, the red one. They made me the neck I wanted and eventually they got the pickup I wanted, which was a humbucker designed by a friend of mine." Ray Butts was the man who designed Gretsch's 'Filtertron' pickup, which was similar in concept to the Gibson humbucker. Previously, Gretsch had been buying in their pickups from the American pickup company DeArmond.

"But the problem was," continues Chet, "there were a couple of guys up there who believed in gimmicks - they were always putting on string mufflers and things like that. They looked at it like designing an automobile, where you had to build in new tricks every year."

And there's that car reference again. But gimmicky or not, the orangey-red 6120 guitar went on to fame and glory, in hindsight at least, because the great Rockabilly guitarist Eddie Cochran always used one - although he improved the sound of his by installing a Gibson P-90 pickup in the neck position. It's unlikely that Gretsch saw much of a boost in sales during Eddie Cochran's tragically short lifetime, but a few years later George Harrison took up a double-cutaway Country Gent and before you could scream, 'Yeah, yeah, yeah,' demand for the guitars went straight through the roof, to the point where Gretsch were soon twelve months behind on their orders. Listen to The Beatles' *All My Loving* to hear how the Gretsch sound complemented George's unorthodox but spirited playing, which itself owed much to that of his idol, Chet Atkins.

Gretsch have made some weird guitars in their time, but perhaps the oddest of all were the ones custom-built for Bo Diddley, whose low-slung oblong-shaped guitars became as much of a trademark as his bizarre rhythm style: "Well, I figured that I'd better come up with something different if I wanted to be noticed," explains the inimitable Bo. "I'd tried Fenders for a while, but the necks were just too thin - Gretsches were the only guitars with necks wide enough for my hands! I used a red Gretsch Jet Firebird on all my early records, but I still wanted a guitar that would really make people sit up and take notice.

"So I took the neck and electrics off a standard Gretsch and put it all onto this square-shaped body. Gretsch also made me some guitars, but they've never been sold to the general public - that

One of the rarest guitars in the world, the fabulous White Penguin

was part of the deal. The very first one they made was shaped like an arrow, but one day I was carrying it on my motorcycle, and I fell off - that was the end of that one!"

But the very characteristics which made Gretsch guitars ideal for rough and ready musical styles, like R&B and early sixties British Beat music, made them very unsuitable indeed for the new wave of high volume Blues that followed soon after, with its emphasis on speed, string-bending and smooth, controllable distortion. Gretsch guitars are generally

Above: Edwyn Collins with Synchromatic acoustic

Below: Close up detail of Gretsch White Falcon

slow players, many of the pickups are underpowered by modern standards, the feedback characteristics tend to be of the undesirable sort and string bending and heavy finger vibrato somehow just don't feel right. So Gretsch began a slow decline both in popularity and quality, and although they soldiered on bravely through the seventies the company eventually went under in 1981.

Ironically, it was at exactly that time that young British post-Punk bands like The Cult, Haircut 100, Spear Of Destiny and Orange Juice rediscovered the cool sounds and cool looks of Gretsch guitars. Like Dave Stewart, The Cult's Billy Duffy loves the Liberace style of the White Falcon.

"Gretsch semi-acoustics aren't the easiest guitars to deal with," says Billy. "The reason I love them is that I've always wanted to get a really heavy guitar sound that's *different*, because so many guitar sounds are the same these days - there's no feel to them.

"My main guitar's a single cutaway White Falcon and I've used that ever since I started. My second guitar is a Gretsch Country Club, and that one isn't quite as good. The thing is, I use loads of harmonics when I play, and the White Falcon's got this high, bent tremolo arm which is great for keeping the feedback down."

There are very, very few players who use Gretsch guitars almost to the exclusion of all others, but one of them is Brian Setzer, a gifted musician who paved the way for the Rockabilly revival of the early eighties with his band The Stray Cats. Brian uses an orange-coloured Gretsch 6120 almost identical to the one that Eddie Cochran employed, and admits that this particular model is essential to the way he plays.

"I actually find that my playing style changes even if I play someone else's Gretsch," laughs Brian. "And if I play a completely different guitar, like my old '59 Les Paul, then it's *really* strange. It doesn't sound bad, but it certainly doesn't sound like me - it's more like Jimmy Page meets Chet Atkins or something!

"I'm something of a Gretsch collector, but the 6120 is my number one guitar. Although it's an old one, it's not the vintage thing that's important to me. If Gretsch could make one now and not lose the magic by messing with it or making the pickups too hot, then I'd use it. I'm not saying all old Gretsches are great because some of them are garbage, but I've yet to play a guitar that will beat my old

Eddie Cochran: his 6120 was fitted with a Gibson P90 pickup

Gretsch; I just plug it into two old Fender Bassman amplifiers and the magic is right there. I must admit I'm really paranoid that it'll get stolen, or that I'll mess it up somehow."

Trying to think of Gretsch guitars which feature in Heavy Rock is not easy. But one Gretsch user is AC/DC's rhythm guitarist Malcolm Young, brother of Angus, the band's *enfant terrible*. Malcolm's double cutaway Jet Firebird has been through the wars - refrets, pickup rewinds, new bridges, etc. - but Young senior won't use anything else: "I've tried to get spare Gretsch Firebirds but they never sound the same," bemoans Malcolm. "This one feels a lot more solid. For some reason it's twice as loud as the others you pick up."

The neck pickup in Young's Gretsch seems to have disappeared; there's a hole where it would normally sit: "That was never used," he states. "It was just a waffly, bassy, middley type of sound that never did anything." Malcolm reckons the modification improved the guitar anyway: "It sounded louder," he affirms.

After a gap of a decade or so out of production, brand-new Gretsch guitars are now back in the shops. They're made partly in Japan and partly in America and although they lack a little of the character of the originals, they're probably better made and hopefully it's a sign that we haven't seen the end of the cowboy jazz guitar yet.

Stray Cats' Brian Setzer toting his 6120

Chapter 9

Guild

The all-round quality American guitar

Founded in the early fifties in New York, Guild boast a history of making guitars ranging in quality from the solid and workmanlike to the very fine indeed. A lot of craftsmen from the original Epiphone company went to work for Guild, and that initially led to the company specialising in Jazz guitars.

Nowadays, though, Guild make all kinds of other guitars as well, including solid electrics, basses, acoustics and acoustic basses. And some of these are very distinguished instruments, especially the

Jazzers and the acoustics. However, Guild's relatively low production figures and low public profile have prevented them from equalling the mainstream status of Gibson, and there's another problem too; anyone with a good ear can identify a Stratocaster, a Telecaster or a Les Paul on a record, but who could put their hand on their heart and swear that a particular screaming solo had emanated from a Guild Bluesbird?

Still, Guild's endorsee list has always been highly impressive. Duane Eddy, the king of twangy Rockabilly guitar, used a fat-bodied Guild with single coil DeArmond pickups, while in more recent times Suzanne Vega, Paul Simon, Johnny Cash and

A pair of Stratford 350s: sunburst and natural

Brian May with his
homemade guitar (left) and
Guild's replica of it (right)

John Denver have all professed themselves to be fans of the powerful sound of Guild's 6- and 12-string acoustic guitars, as has Eric Clapton who, after all, can play anything he pleases. And there's a surprisingly large contingent from the rockier end of the scale using Guild's slimline electro-acoustics, including Slash from Guns N'Roses and Aerosmith's Joe Perry.

Even Brian Setzer, guitarist with Rockabilly revivalists The Stray Cats, occasionally forsakes his vintage Gretsch for a Guild electric, while the hugely charismatic Chicago Bluesman Buddy Guy has always alternated between the wild, wiry sound of a Fender Strat and the raunchier, more powerful response of his old Guild Starfire semi-acoustic, a guitar not dissimilar to a Gibson ES335.

One of the most interesting instruments Guild have made has been a copy of Brian May's famous home-made guitar. "Guild's craftsmanship is really second to none," said Brian of his original Guild signature model. "I've been to the factory a few

Above: Twin cutaway Starfire
Left: Duane Eddy, king of the twang!

times and it's all done by hand, instead of being sent off to Japan or Korea with the plans.

"They built it out of solid mahogany, while mine is actually blockboard - real rubbish! So the Guilds are a little heavier and they've slightly slimmed down the neck on the production models, because mine is really thick and wide, and not many people apart from myself would like it. They've also changed the old Burns Tri-Sonic pickups for DiMarzios, which sound very close, and they've put on a proper Kahler tremolo system but altered it to feel like mine. And it's been great to have a spare guitar after all this time, because although I can play Fenders and Gibsons at home, they just don't do what I want them to do on stage."

Since Brian spoke those words the original Guild Brian May model has been discontinued and a new version released. The new guitar is, in some ways, closer to the May model than Guild's first attempt, having changed to Seymour Duncan pickups and incorporated a tremolo system more akin to Brian's own.

Guild are famous for their acoustic guitars; this one is a D4

Chapter 10

Hofner

German suppliers to the British Beat boom

Among the impoverished Beat groups playing the German clubs and USAF bases in the late fifties and early sixties, the quest was to find an affordable European version of a famous American guitar. The Hofner company of Bubenreuth provided the answer, echoing as they did the designs of Kalamazoo's finest, to the point where their guitars were frequently dubbed the 'Gibsons of Europe'.

Although signature guitars proliferate nowadays, in the late fifties one of the most popular British guitarists, Bert Weedon, had a 'signature' guitar: a hollow-bodied electric Golden Hofner; so called because of its distinctively-coloured maple veneers and use of gold-plated hardware.

The Committee, a similar instrument to the Golden, was designed around 1959, by a 'committee' of six guitarists, including Weedon, and found use with guitarists such as Denny Wright, who played guitar for Skiffle star Lonnie Donegan.

Hofner's Club series (40, 50 and 60) provided a unique niche for the company; these hollow-bodied models lay somewhere in size between Gibson's Les Paul and archtop L-5, and were particularly attractive in their own way.

The most famous Hofner user, of course, was The Beatles' Paul McCartney, with his 500/1 Violin bass.

President and Beatle basses

Hofner's premier model, the Golden

The bass was a hollow-bodied instrument, similar in appearance but radically different from Gibson's commercially doomed EB-1, which was actually made from solid mahogany. Frequently referred to as the 'Beatle Bass', Hofner issued the instrument (once The Beatles had become famous) with a tag showing a smiling Paul McCartney giving his ubiquitous 'thumbs-up' to the happy purchaser.

Top of the Club range, the ornate Club 60

The other guitar playing Beatles also had Hofners. McCartney has been quoted as saying that both John and George probably purchased Club models - at Steinway's shop, where Paul's first Beatle Bass was obtained - while the band were gigging in Hamburg.

There was a fifth Beatle, too, the enigmatic Stuart Sutcliffe who played, or at least owned, a brunette President bass. Sutcliffe attempted the role of bassist in The Beatles before it was realised he had no real musical aptitude. He was, however, an extraordinary artist and bought his bass with the money he'd received from the sale of a painting.

Many of the British groups played Hofners. Indeed, Pink Floyd's guitarist Dave Gilmour owned a Club 60 as his first guitar; Ritchie Blackmore of Deep Purple was another Club user; the Moody Blues' guitarist Justin Hayward played a Hofner Club before trading up to a Gibson ES335; and Roy Wood of the Move and later ELO, played more than one Hofner solid before purchasing a pink Fender Stratocaster.

And thereby hangs the tail. Hofner guitars, despite the fondness with which they are recalled by their early players, were unfortunately seen as stepping stones to Gibsons or Fenders, such was the charisma of these sought-after American instru-ments. Due to their weak pickups, idiosyncratic control arrangements and fragile construction, Hofners are rarely played by top bands today, although Paul McCartney sometimes still uses his Beatle Bass; and Luke Haines, guitarist with Indie band The Auteurs, remains faithful to a late sixties Committee.

The Hofner company still builds guitars today and since the sixties has produced a whole array of models, from the Strat-styled Galaxie to the 335-ish Verithin, and literally hundreds of other designs. But it's the classic Hofners of the fifties and sixties which are now becoming collectable and beginning to fetch prices which, even a few years ago, would have been unthinkable.

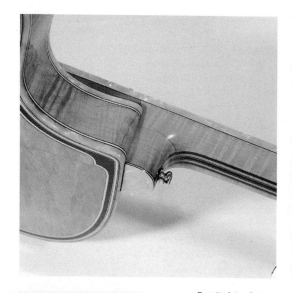

Detail of the Golden Hofner's craftsmanship

The Club 50: this was the first good guitar for many of today's stars

Chapter 11

Ibanez

Japanese success story of the eighties

The Japanese Ibanez company has managed to amass one of the most impressive endorser lists of any guitar manufacturer. Ibanez players include some of the best known guitarists in the business, from Jazz players like George Benson and Joe Pass to modern Rock guitar idols such as Steve Vai and Joe Satriani, as well as sophisticated singer-songwriters like Joni Mitchell.

The involvement of the artist with the company in developing an instrument to suit his or her requirements has invariably prompted Ibanez to produce a model bearing the musician's name. For instance, after a long period of research and development the Joe Satriani model was designed, using features from other guitars which Joe has enjoyed playing: "I like the contour of a sixties Fender neck," says Joe. "And I like small frets, low to the fretboard - I like the worn out feel." Satriani has his Floyd Rose tremolo arm set so that it feels light, using only two springs as opposed to the more usual three or four to counteract the tension of the strings and balance the system. He also likes the unit sunk into the guitar's top, so the strings run low over the body: "It's like a cross between the Stratocaster and Les Paul, as far as the height

Ibanez's now famous headstock design

between the strings and the guitar go," he maintains.

Joe, however, has recently collaborated with Ibanez to produce a guitar which goes completely against the grain of modern Rock playing - it has no tremolo arm! "When you use a vibrato bar guitar," explains Joe, "when you hit the strings really hard, a lot of the vibration gets transferred to the springs and back into the bar in a sort of 'flutter' and I don't like that sound at all.

Brian May with his Ibanez JS: a gift from Joe Satriani himself

One of the company's prime endorsers, Joe Satriani

and it's exactly what I want to see. Fortunately they made it available for people and it sold a lot better than I thought it would." Steve asked for seven hundred and seventy seven of the green Jem guitars to be made: "I signed every one of them and they're all sold," he says, with obvious satisfaction.

Vai then designed a 7-string guitar which Ibanez put straight onto the market under the name Universe UV7. This guitar carried a £1025 price tag when it was launched in the summer of 1990.

While Ibanez have achieved the highest of profiles through their work with the stars of Rock guitar, they have also made a considerable mark in the world of Jazz, with their George Benson and Joe Pass models.

The George Benson GB10 takes its influence

Ibanez has worked with me to try to get as little flutter as possible, by using certain springs or arrangements of springs."

So Joe spoke to his favourite luthier, Gary Brawer from San Fransicsco, and together they came up with the solution: a regular, Gibson-style stud tailpiece, but made by pickup manufacturer DiMarzio. Joe: "It was perfect for me because a lot of the finger vibrato that I had developed over the years suddenly sounded more like me, because the vibrato bar wasn't there taking up the slack and giving way every time I applied finger vibrato. And when I hit those chords really hard there was none of that fluttering noise and so the rhythm parts became a little spankier sounding. We wound up using that guitar for *Friends, The Extremist, War,* and *Motorcycle Driver.*"

One of Satriani's former pupils is rock guitar hero Steve Vai, another Ibanez endorser. Vai's wacky ideas have often stretched the company's research and development department to its limit, although the heart-shaped, triple-necked instrument which Steve has used live was never destined for production.

But one guitar which did get into limited production was the Jem 777. Although relatively conventional in appearance this guitar defied convention by the inclusion of a carrying handle in the top of the body, a feature which Vai patented. Talking about the Jem 777 Steve points out, "It's my design. Along with Ibanez I constructed the guitar

Steve Vai's 7-string Universe guitar

The number one Ibanez player, Steve Vai

from Gibson's famous Jazz guitars, although it is considerably smaller than an L-5 or ES175. It first appeared in 1977 and featured a spruce top with maple back and sides. A special plate with the name George Benson was inlaid at the 21st fret and the guitar boasted two floating pickups attached to the pickguard. Ibanez have produced two other Benson models; a larger bodied GB20 with a single pickup and pickguard-mounted controls, and an Anniversary model which was issued in 1990.

When Ibanez approached Jazz legend Joe Pass and offered to make him a guitar Joe jumped at the chance, and was knocked out with the results: "I simply told them what I liked in a neck and how I liked the action and so on. They make very good guitars; the workmanship is far better than any workmanship, it's sad to say, on any American guitar I've tried".

Another Ibanez player is ex-Miles Davis guitarist John Scofield. Scofield prefers the slimmer, semi-acoustic AS-200 Artist model - based loosely on Gibson's ES300 series - to the bigger-bodied guitars favoured by Pass and Benson.

A fine player who thinks even thinner than

The Jem 777: one of only 777 made

Scofield is Frank Gambale, who holds down one of Jazz's most demanding gigs, with Chick Corea's Elektric Band. Frank worked with Ibanez to produce the wafer-slim Sabre model, fitted with DiMarzio Super Distortion pickups and making it seem more at home in Heavy Metal than on a Jazz Fusion bandstand. Frank, however, had definite ideas about the guitar he wanted: "I had them make me one out of mahogany. I'm crazy over mahogany and I had a sound in my head that I was going for with this guitar. Ibanez also made me another one which is different. They've lined up the fretboard flush with the body and it's even thinner than the first Sabre - I really hate that block at the heel of the guitar and on this new model it's been reduced so much it's almost not there..."

Queen's Brian May is another recent Ibanez convert. Although not relegating his home-made 'special' to the scrap heap, Brian has been enjoying the use of a Satriani model Ibanez which, apparently, Joe arranged for him with the company. Brian speaks highly of the instrument: "It's really inspiring and also speedy up the top end of the neck."

Ibanez' strategy of advertisements prominently featuring the company's artists, together with a policy of continual research and development into exactly what the player wants, has shown that there is room, even in a market overcrowded with products, for one more success story.

John Scofield: one of a growing number of Jazzers to favour Ibanez

Chapter 12

Jackson/Charvel

Def Leppard: Phil Collen (centre) plays both Jackson and Charvel

Purveyors of guitars to Rock's gentry

From a small guitar repair and modification company in California, started by Wayne Charvel and Grover Jackson, Jackson/Charvel grew in a matter of a decade into one of the biggest guitar companies in the world, producing custom and mass-produced instruments both in the USA and the Far East. They quickly captured a large slice of the Rock market when the fashion for fast, exotic guitars began to grow in the early eighties.

The models in the Jackson/Charvel range fitted the requirements of the Metal and Thrash brigade exactly. These flashy players took to the aggressive pointed headstocks, the two octave necks and the deep cutaways immediately. The success of Jackson/Charvel was simply a matter of producing the right guitars at the right time.

In terms of appearance and sound Jackson/Charvel guitars look not unlike hot-rodded Fenders, with their bolt-on maple necks and

Not just manic Rock guitars – this Charvel Surfcaster features a heavy retro theme

vaguely Strat-like bodies; their sound, though, is a good cross between Gibson and Fender, the instruments often having a powerful humbucking pickup by the bridge and two slimmer, and thinner-sounding, Strat-style units in the middle and neck positions.

One long-time Jackson devotee is Anthrax guitarist Danny Spitz. Danny explains that although Jackson have a large endorsee list they don't give guitars away just because a player is famous. "A lot of big name players who use Jacksons actually buy them," he announces, "but they don't mind paying the bucks because they're such great guitars."

Spitz' own reason for endorsing Jacksons goes back long before he joined Anthrax. "I've been playing them for years now and I used to buy them before I got an endorsement deal with the company. They're pretty expensive guitars compared to some, but they're worth the money because of their quality, playability and sound."

All of Danny's Jacksons have the sharkfin body that Ozzy Osbourne's late lamented guitarist, Randy Rhoads, helped develop - but with a difference. "Although all of my bodies are the Randy Rhoads model shape, they're slightly smaller then usual. I'm pretty small and for this reason I've

Under all this hair is Jackson-lover, Dave Mustaine of Megadeth

Anthrax's Scott Ian – Jacksons are firm favourites with the Thrash brigade

Below: The handsome bass version of the Surfcaster

Jackson/Charvel's sculpted heel assists top fret access

always had Jackson cut the size of the body down."

Another respected player who enthuses equally about Jackson guitars is Phil Collen of Def Leppard. "Grover Jackson sent me one and it blew me away completely," says Phil. "I then met Grover in person and he made me a Soloist with Jackson pickups in it and a Kahler tremolo and I fell in love with the thing straight away. They've built me a specially shaped guitar with a 24 fret neck and they've also given me one that glows in the dark, which is quite novel - looks great with the lights off."

Thrash band Megadeth's two guitarists, Dave Mustaine and Marty Friedman, are both committed Jackson players. Friedman has collaborated with Jackson on the design of a 'Marty Friedman' signature model. This guitar, with its vaguely Explorer-shaped body and headstock is all black and features Jackson's famous 'sharkfin'

Dramatic finishes have always been part of the Jackson image

Right: The Jackson Randy Rhoads: a tribute to the late great guitarist

fingerboard inlays, but no tremolo system. Friedman: "I don't like the sound of a tremolo bar. All the vibrato I want I can do with my fingers and I despise the sound of dive-bombs and squeals. To me, that sort of whammy bar stuff is a total waste of space in your solo and I can't validate that. To be frank, I've never found a space in a lead break where I've felt like using a whammy bar."

While the company name is Jackson/Charvel the guitars are marketed separately under both names, at the top of the pile sitting the Jackson Professional, USA and Custom Shop models.

As well as their standard 6-strings and basses Jackson also produce a limited number of twin-necked guitars, an instrument which appeals to Canadian Blues guitarist Jeff Healey. Healey, who is blind, plays the instrument in the most unusual way; sitting down and resting it on his knees, rather like a lap steel player. He says of his Jackson twin-neck, "I bought one in Los Angeles. It's a beautiful thing and it has the best 12-string neck on it that I've ever experienced on any guitar. I could play both necks at the same time - if I had four hands!"

Above: A range of American and Japanese Jacksons in a variety of wild finishes

Chapter 13

The jazz guitarists

Django, the greatest Jazz guitarist of them all?

Masters of musical invention

Few Jazz guitarists achieve the kind of household fame enjoyed by even minor league pop artists, but no book dealing with star guitars and star guitarists would be complete without a look, however brief and incomplete, at the history of the Jazz guitar. If you want to be exact, there's really no such thing as a 'Jazz' guitar - you can play any style of music on any style of guitar you please. Some Jazz musicians use classical guitars, some use acoustic guitars, some use solid electric guitars, but 'Jazz guitar' still means a certain type of instrument and the leader in the design and manufacture of jazz guitars has always been Gibson.

It was Orville Gibson himself who invented the archtop guitar, and Gibson legend Lloyd Loar who turned it into the cello guitar, or orchestra guitar, or f-hole guitar, now the accepted standard for Jazz players. Eddie Lang, a true pioneer of the genre, used various acoustic Gibsons including the top-of-the-range L5. But for a long time the guitar was second to the banjo in the field of Jazz, and for a simple reason: guitars simply didn't have enough volume to be heard over trumpets, saxophones and drums, despite the ever-increasing size of the orchestra guitar. And it was not until the invention of the magnetic pickup in the thirties that guitars had a chance to be properly heard.

Gibson didn't make the world's first electric guitar but it was nevertheless an electric ES150 model which found fame with one of the guitar's first true superstars, Charlie Christian. Although Charlie Christian wasn't the first guitarist ever to record with the electric guitar, it was Christian who did more than anyone else to help lift the guitar from its role as a pure rhythm instrument into a new realm of melody. And although he died tragically young, in his twenties, just like Eddie Lang, he had done enough in that time to ensure that guitar playing would never be the same again.

With a range of guitars from the affordable to the magnificent - like the L5 and the gigantic Super 400 - Gibson easily hung on to their reputation as the makers of the finest jazz guitars right through the forties, fifties and sixties, and their catalogues boasted a galaxy of stars who endorsed their instruments. They also introduced a number of 'signature' guitars including the Howard Roberts, the Johnny Smith, the Barney Kessel and the Tal Farlow (the latter still uses his 1964 Tal Farlow model, but Kessel has long since reverted to his ES150). Other great Gibson players have included Joe Pass, Herb Ellis and Pat Metheny, all ES175 fanciers, and Wes Montgomery; even Derek Bailey, a Jazz experimenter light years away from Eddie Lang, extracts his unlikely sounds from a traditional Gibson archtop.

Of course, Gibsons aren't the only Jazz guitars in existence, and other companies have made superlative instruments, even if they never achieved the same following. Fender, for instance, never succeeded in making a successful Jazz guitar, although they tried. From the thirties to the fifties Epiphone followed close on Gibson's heels with many superb Jazzers; Freddie Green, rhythm guitarist with Count Basie, always played an Epiphone.

Guild Jazz guitars did well

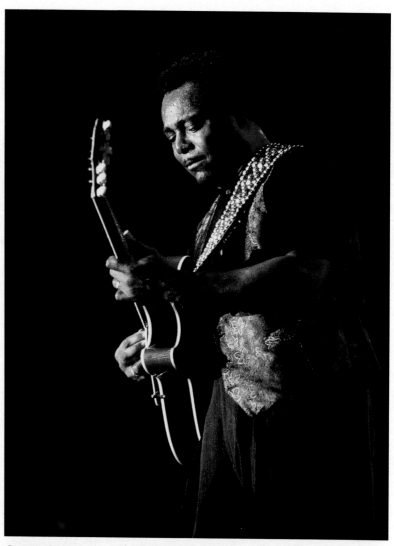

Sometime Pop star: the gifted guitarist, George Benson

Barney Kessel, who doesn't play a Gibson Barney Kessel!

One of the American Jazz masters, Tal Farlow

in the late fifties and early sixties; George Barnes played a Guild, and so did Johnny Smith before he switched his allegiance to Gibson. Gretsch Jazz guitars were considered too coarse by many players, although Sal Salvador played one, and so did the 7-string wizard George Van Eps. Many famous players, like Charlie Byrd and Jim Hall, have used guitars by the great New York maker D'Angelico and his successor D'Aquisto; D'Angelicos are currently some of the most valuable guitars on the collector's market, selling for many thousands of pounds.

But as the fifties waned so did the demand for Jazz, and it wasn't until the seventies and the birth of Jazz/Rock or 'Fusion' that players once again sought the warmth and the human quality of the semi-acoustic guitar. Gibson's thinline guitars (hybrids like the ES335, invented in 1958 and crossing Les Pauls with 'real' Jazz guitars) became all the rage. Larry Carlton, Lee Ritenour and John Scofield all used them, and your average seventies session musician would be more likely to leave his shoes behind than his trusty 335!

The seventies also saw the coming-of-age of the Japanese guitar, and soon Ibanez, Yamaha and Aria were all producing good instruments, some of them fine enough to rival their American competitors. George Benson has consistently used the signature guitar that Ibanez designed for him, the George Benson GB-10; Herb Ellis forsook his

Pat Metheny, who bridges the gap between Jazz and Rock as successfully as anyone

Herb Ellis, whose Gibson ES175 has accompanied many of the greats, including Ella Fitzgerald and Oscar Peterson

Gibson for the Aria PE175, for a while at least, and Martin Taylor, currently one of the finest Jazz players around, will rarely be seen with anything but a Yamaha.

We should also mention the Jazz guitar's honourable role in Rock and Roll history. Scotty Moore, Elvis Presley's innovative guitarist, relied upon a Gibson L5 and his famous gold-coloured Gibson ES295, while Chuck Berry often used a lower-grade version of the L5 called the ES350. Bill Haley, whose guitarist in the Comets, Danny Cidrone (better known for his black Gibson Les Paul) would often hang a Gibson Super 400 round his neck. And Eddie Cochran's wielding of a Gretsch 6120 single-handedly transformed this Jazz instrument into a Rock and Roll guitar.

Many rock guitarists have taken a strong fancy to Gibson's workhorse Jazz guitar, the ES175 - Yes's Steve Howe in particular - while wild-haired rocker Ted Nugent always plays a similar specification but physically scaled down version of the L5, the fabulous Gibson Byrdland.

But as you can see by Gibson's dominance of this chapter, Jazz guitarists are sometimes just as keen to be seen with the 'right' guitar as players in any other genre. There are some notable exceptions though. Jim Mullen, of course, plays a guitar that most people would associate with Country or Rock and Roll - a Fender Telecaster. For a long time John McLaughlin used a guitar which, although a Gibson, was bizarre by anyone's standards - it had a separate row of 'drone' strings which vibrated in sympathy with the normal strings.

And one of the finest musicians this century has seen, the great gypsy guitarist Django Reinhardt who died in 1953, used a revolutionary kind of acoustic called a Maccaferri. These guitars were built in Paris in the thirties and easily distinguished by their D-shaped or oval soundholes. The loud volume and sharp attack of this unusual guitar suited Django perfectly; on a visit to America he was forced to play a Gretsch - a good Jazz guitar by anyone else's standards - but Django detested it!

Chapter 14

Martin

Inventors of the acoustic guitar as we know it

There are hundreds and hundreds of different makes of acoustic guitars, but virtually all of them owe something to the Martin company of Nazareth, Pennsylvania, who have spent more than a hundred and fifty years making perhaps the best-respected acoustics in the world.

It's absolutely impossible to name all the famous musicians who have played Martin guitars, because they've *all* used them! Bob Dylan, Ry Cooder, Elvis Presley, Jimi Hendrix, Paul Simon, Hank Williams, Eric Clapton, Joni Mitchell, James Taylor, Crosby, Stills, Nash and Young, Richard Thompson, Paul McCartney, and more great country musicians than you could shake a stick at have relied upon Martins at one time or another. And if you go into any guitar shop and pick out any acoustic guitar, whether it be from the West or the East, the odds are that it's a copy or a near copy of a design originated by Martin over seventy years ago. While this is a great tribute to the originators of the designs, it makes it difficult to recognise when someone's playing the genuine article - unless you're close enough to the stage to read the script on the headstock - which must be a great source of annoyance to Martin themselves.

The company was founded in 1833 when Christian Friedrich Martin moved from the violin-making town of

Markneukirchen in Saxony to New York, and from there, five years later, to the Nazareth district; the company grew gradually from a tiny business to one that employed 75 people in 1925, and while Martin's earlier instruments were all gut-strung models, by the end of the twenties they'd moved

Two of Mark Knopfler's vintage Martins

Two Martin dreadnoughts flanking an 00 Model

almost completely to making steel-strung guitars.

Along the way Martin have made a number of innovations that are now accepted practice among all guitar-makers. They were the first to use 'X-bracing', a system of reinforcing the belly of the instrument with struts laid in the shape of a cross; they were the first to make guitars with necks that joined the body at the fourteenth fret, as opposed to the twelfth; and they invented the 'Dreadnought'

guitar, an extra-large size of instrument which has achieved the rare state of being so incredibly popular that it's virtually unnoticeable - it's just 'an acoustic guitar'.

Modern Martin guitars are excellent instruments, but you'll still hear players going on about 1941 D-45s, 1935 D-28s and so on. Certain old Martins are worth a lot of money, and they're worth even more if they've had a famous owner. Jimi Hendrix used to hammer for one hundred and eighty thousand dollars - enough to buy over a hundred brand-new ones!

Like many American companies Martin had their period of producing, if not inferior instruments then let's say indifferent ones. Indifferent for them that is. Though not entirely the fault of the manufacturers themselves - most of the blame can go on the sheer quantities demanded in the late sixties and

The keenly priced 00016

Believe it or not, this was Jimi Hendrix's favourite guitar. Here is Mitch Mitchell with Jimi's D45

own a Martin D-45, their top-of-the-line Dreadnought model with yards of real abalone pearl inlay around the edges, around the soundhole and up the neck and headstock. It's been owned since 1971 by Mitch Mitchell, drummer with the Jimi Hendrix Experience, who tells how Jimi kept it propped up in a corner of his London flat, ready to be played in moments of inspiration. This guitar was therefore the likely starting place for many a Hendrix classic. And although Hendrix owned a number of acoustic guitars, including a 12-string and an Epiphone given to him by his friend Stephen Stills, this one was his absolute favourite.

You might think that if this guitar ever came up for auction it would be the most expensive Martin ever sold, but it would have to beat the amazing price paid for Elvis Presley's battered old D-18. Elvis used this Martin throughout the early part of his career - that's the guitar you hear on songs like *That's Alright Mama* and *Mystery Train* - and although he sold the instrument to one of his neighbours in 1956, it recently went under the

A modern classic from Martin: a J40M in unusual black finish

throughout the seventies - there was however a feeling in the marketplace that Fender, Gibson, Martin etc. thought they could get away with churning out more or less anything.

It was during this time that the Japanese got their initial foothold on the market, and their tenacity, together with the fact that these instruments weren't half bad, ensured their continued success.

While companies like Takamine, Aria and Washburn began by producing Martin lookalikes (they were never to Martin's standard due to their laminated - in other words plywood - construction) they now all produce original instruments of extremely high quality. The Eurythmics' Dave Stewart is a confirmed Takamine player and says of his instruments: "Takamine acoustics... are just brilliant. Playing on stage is amazing, given the problems you usually have with acoustics. These have the EQ (equalisiation - sophisticated tone control) and you just get the perfect acoustic guitar sound, without sounding electric. When we do the six numbers acoustically - songs like *You Have Placed A Chill In My Heart* - the sound out of the P.A. is just crystal clear."

Chapter 15

Music Man

Modern masterpieces in the Californian tradition

In 1965, when Leo Fender sold out to the giant CBS Corporation for $13,000,000, part of the agreement was that he would not participate in any musical venture for ten years, even though CBS kept him on as a consultant for some time thereafter.

So a decade later Leo bought into Music Man, a company which had itself been set up by former Fender men, Forrest White and Tom Walker. Leo immediately set about designing two new Music Man guitars; first the Sting Ray and then the Sabre. These instruments were distinctly 'Fender-like' in both construction and appearance, featuring screw-on necks with a mechanical tilt adjustment - actually an improved version of the one Leo had designed for CBS! Sales of the Sabre and Sting Ray, however, failed to meet the levels of expectation that their quality - and of course the Fender connection - had led people to believe would follow.

But among the disappointments there was a success story. Leo's Sting Ray bass quickly found favour among a new generation of players who, in contrast to their more conservative 6-string counterparts, were beginning to take notice of such advances as onboard active electronics, which greatly enhanced an instrument's tonal response and range.

Among the many fine players who switched to the Sting Ray from their Precisions and Jazzes, Paul Young's distinctive fretless bassist Pino Palladino probably epitomises the Music Man user. "I tried it out and it said 'yes' to me," says Palladino, simply. Pino likes his fretless Sting Ray because it feels solid, dependable and familiar: "They're great basses, I love the sound. They are quite close to a Fender - in fact they're just like an antique Fender - but they do have a sound of their own."

In 1980 Leo went off to form G&L with his old Fender compatriot George Fullerton, and Music Man was purchased by guitar string manufacturing giant Ernie Ball.

Ball's son Sterling is Vice President of the company and also best friend of country picker supreme, Albert Lee. So it's hardly surprising that Albert is now a confirmed Music Man user. Albert's unusual angular guitar (a left-handed version of

which Paul McCartney also enjoys playing) is one that was initially designed to be built in Canada and the Far East: "But they're a fiercely American company and decided against that," said Albert. "Anyway, I'd seen one at the factory and thought it looked alright, then I went and played at the Ernie

Albert Lee, with his Music Man signature model

Nigel Tufnel of Spinal Tap – the speedo works and the position markers are numbered musically!

Ball Christmas party and Sterling said, 'I've got a new guitar... when you see it you'll want it.' And he opened the case and I saw this beautiful pink thing with a birdseye maple neck and I thought, 'God, I want it!' and Sterling said, 'You can have it.'"

As well as Albert Lee, Music Man have picked up some of the biggest names in Rock and Roll. "Keith Richards has been using one, and enjoying it too -

not just having his picture taken with it," continues Albert Lee.

In 1990 Music Man signed up Edward Van Halen and together they designed Eddie's ultimate guitar: "The body is basswood and comes with either a bound flamed maple top or a bound quilted maple top. The guitar has a 22 fret maple neck. I hope people check it out and see just how much thought and time has gone into it."

Ernie Ball Music Man are one of the hungry new breed of American companies who have plugged the gaps which the two big names, Fender and Gibson, have failed to fill. Their concentration on good design, low output and high quality should ensure that Edward Van Halen's summary of his Music Man 'signature' guitar comes true: "I think it's the kind of guitar that, ten years down the road, people are gonna go, 'Woa! Man, this is a really nice axe'. I think it will stand the test of time."

Although Van Halen is now happily signed to Ernie Ball Music Man it's worth noting Edward's influence over modern playing. He was one of the first players to defy convention and fit a fat sounding humbucking pickup in the bridge position of his Stratocaster, because the rest of the band said it was too thin-sounding.

"I said, 'Okay, I'll take care of that.' I put a humbucker in there and figured out how to wire up the rest of it. I just chiselled a hole in the body and thought, 'Hey, this is neat.' It was like, 'You can't buy one of these' and I felt like I was on to something - obviously I was!"

Between his home-made humbucking Strat and his Music Man signature guitar Eddie changed to Kramer who, at the time of writing, are no longer producing guitars. Along with Travis Bean, Kramer had been at the leading edge of seventies aluminium neck technology, until lack of sales proved that the public wasn't yet ready for such advances. So Kramer went the way of so many other manufacturers and put together their version of a hot-rodded Strat-style guitar, and for a while Van Halen was the company's prime endorser. "I just like their guitars," he said at the time; "I play one all the time now."

A third guitar built around the 'Albert Lee' Model is a most curious example, especially put together by Music Man for Spinal Tap's Nigel Tufnel, perhaps rock music's most enigmatic character. As well as a paint job worthy of any hotrod, Nigel's guitar sports four humbucking pickups, a set of exhaust pipes and a working speedometer!

"It's my design," states Nigel, proudly. "You see the inverted letters, G, A, C#? It's so you know where you are all the time. The tremolo is a Floyd Rose and the arm is a Hearst Shifter, with the 8-ball on the end. The chrome pipes are called Headers and the picture is

Above: Eddie Van Halen tapping out a melody on his Music Man EVH

Below: A multi-coloured line-up of Van Halen models

'Mr Horsepower' from the fifties. The control knob is a Goodyear tyre and of course the lights light up and the speedo works and lights up as well."

Although keen on his guitar's motor sport theme, it's the pickups which Nigel is really excited about: "The outer ones are Van Halens, one is a DiMarzio PAF and one's a Fred, because Joe Satriani gave me an Ibanez guitar as a gift for Christmas and I liked the sound of it (the Fred is a pickup designed by Satriani and DiMarzio). It took a month to build, but I've got one of those fax machines, you know, so they would draw a picture and send it to me and I would send it back and back and back. A man named Dudley Gimpel at Music Man made it and he's a genius."

The excellent silhouette from Ernie Ball/Music Man

A brace of Sting Ray basses: one fretted, the other fretless

Chapter 16

National/Dobro

Metal monsters or music's missing link?

On the sleeve of one of the best-selling albums of recent years, Dire Straits' 'Brothers In Arms', is an example of what are possibly the wildest and most eye-catching guitars ever made. Silhouetted against the sky, it looks something like an acoustic guitar and yet seems to be covered entirely in chrome, highly polished and lavishly engraved with a Hawaiian beach scene, complete with palm trees!

But despite the almost futuristic looks, the guitar pictured on the sleeve is Mark Knopfler's own National guitar, an instrument which dates not from the seventies, nor from the sixties, but from the late 1930s - and you couldn't even call this one an early example of its type, since similar guitars were being made a decade earlier.

The proper name for these extraordinary instruments is 'resonator guitars' and they form a fascinating chapter in the history of the guitar because the theory behind them is fundamentally different from that of any other guitar ever made.

Although invented in Los Angeles by a Czechoslovakian immigrant called John Dopyera - who in 1925 founded a company called the National String Instrument Corporation - resonator guitars were soon being manufactured under a bewildering number of brand names. But whatever the name on the headstock, the basic principle remained the same - the vibrations from the strings were transferred, through the bridge, to either one

The Notting Hillbillies' Nationals

The Notting Hillbillies and their guitars

or three aluminium speaker cones located within the instrument's body.

The aim, of course, was to make a guitar louder than any yet invented, because as bands in the twenties and early thirties became bigger and increasingly louder, the low-volume acoustic guitar was in severe danger of being overwhelmed to the point of being inaudible. Guitar players battled with this in several ways, either by using big-bodied orchestra guitars or by switching to banjo when the going got rough, but the hard, metallic sound of the resonators succeeded in cutting through where all-wood guitars had failed. And, from the visual side of things, they were stunning creations, some with brightly-painted wooden bodies, others with all-metal bodies with finishes that ranged from the plain, galvanised type to exotic silver or even gold-plating, covered with intricate floral or art deco motifs.

Although nowadays we usually associate these guitars with old-time Blues musicians, in actual fact Nationals and Dobros (Dobro being an abbreviation of Dopyera Brothers) were widely used both as rhythm guitars in the pre-electric era Jazz bands

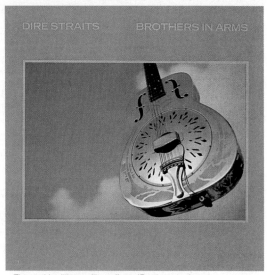

The multi-million selling album 'Brothers In Arms'

and as 'steel' guitars in Country music, where the musician held the instrument horizontally in the Hawaiian style and used a 'steel', or metal bar, to play single or double-note accompaniments. But it's true that the resonator guitar found its real niche with the black Blues musicians of the Mississippi Delta, who often tuned their guitars to a chord and placed the neck from a glass bottle over one of their fingers to produce the most lonely and evocative music ever created.

American guitarist Bob Brozman has built a life around the music of National guitars. The bearded, bespectacled and eccentric Brozman dresses in thirties-style suits and dickie bow ties and plays a variety of single cone and tricone Nationals, as well as mandolins and ukuleles also made by the company. He bought his first National when he was only eighteen. "I was home from university when I found a Triplate in a music store in New York," recollects Brozman, who didn't have enough money for the guitar and was unable to persuade the store to hold it for him. "So I had a friend break into my apartment back in St Louis and bring me my two regular guitars so that I could trade them in." While waiting for these guitars to arrive, Bob took the train from Long Island to New York every day for two weeks, just to make sure he wasn't beaten to the

Plastic-bodied National Glenwood

Relation to the Nationals: the wooden-bodied Dobro

purchase. "I just sat in the corner of the store with the guitar, not letting anyone else touch it."

Brozman finds it worrisome transporting these priceless instruments around the world, since the occasional mishap is bound to occur. "My Triplate's had the neck broken twice," admits Bob, "once by the airlines and once when I was on my way to record my first album for Kicking Mule records. I was riding in a Volkswagen when I got hit head on by a police car. I broke my back, which put me out of commission for a year - and also the headstock on my National got busted!"

Such tragedies aside, Brozmen tells two stories which detail the inherent toughness of these guitars: "I once saw a National that had a bullet hole in the front and only a bump in the back. The bullet didn't go all the way through and the guitar obviously saved the guy's life!" Another incident occurred when Brozman was playing in the notoriously tough town of Florence, Arizona: "I was standing up playing my guitar when this really drunk guy came over and just grabbed all six strings and started to tug. I knew he'd have destroyed the guitar if he'd continued, so in a fit of unusual bravery I swung and knocked him in the stomach with the neck. As he bent forwards I unhooked the strap from the body and whacked him on the side of his head with the guitar, which knocked him out cold." Apparently the guitar remained intact, although Bob decided that discretion was the better part of valour: "I made sure I was out of town before he woke up!"

Since resonator guitars produced their sound by mechanical means, they could almost be dubbed the missing link between the acoustic steel-strung guitar and the electrically amplified instruments of today. But this also meant that their heyday lasted only until the widespread availability of electric guitars, when the National company concentrated increasingly on solid-bodied 'lap steel' guitars and, in the fifties and sixties, wild-shaped electrics that made extensive use of plastic in their construction.

However, the folk blues revival of the sixties led to a new appreciation of these strange guitars, and players like Crosby Stills and Nash's Steve Stills were quick to exploit their sound and image. The nineties see National and Dobro back in full swing, making reproductions of their classic early designs.

These days, resonator guitars often turn up as props for Pop videos and, less frequently, on the actual records themselves. But The Kinks' *Lola* is a good example of a resonator guitar on record, as is *Romeo And Juliet* by Dire Straits, and there's now an up-and-coming National user in the shape of American singer Chris Whitley.

But Mark Knopfler is perhaps the most prominent ambassador for these guitars; in pre-Straits days he played with a blues band called the Duolian String Pickers (a 'Duolian' is a cheap Dobro model) and in fact his side-project The Notting Hillbillies based their whole public image around them. Steve Phillips from that band is something of a National connoisseur: "The first time I saw one was in a picture of Bukka White" (bottleneck blues great, and a relative of B.B. King). "I just thought, 'What *is* that thing?' They're great because they're so alien-looking, with the way the light reflects off them. I got my first one for £25 and I've had a few others since then. I'm sure every National ever built is still being played somewhere, because they're virtually indestructable! The ultimate National must be the one that Tampa Red was reputed to own, which was probably a gold-plated Tri-plate with three resonators. It must have looked absolutely amazing!"

All Knopfler has to say about his National is that it's so old that it's doing it no favours dragging it around the world. On the other hand, with the profits from 'Brothers In Arms' alone he could probably afford to buy a different National for every day of the year.

Chapter 17

Ovation

Bringing the acoustic guitar to the stadium stage

Like hundreds upon hundreds of star guitar players, Bon Jovi's lead instrumentalist Richie Sambora loves Ovations. Hardly surprising, though, when you consider what they made for him: a triple-necked 6-string, 12-string and mandolin. In fact they built him a pair of them!

"I wanted to incorporate a mandolin," explains Sambora. "I do this suite of different acoustic pieces with a piece on the mandolin. Then I drop down a neck and do a very flamenco-ish, western thing on the 6-string, and I open up *Wanted* on the 12-string, like I do on the record." But when Sambora first approached Ovation with his idea their immediate response was that it was unfeasible; the tensions involved were far too great. But Sambora was not to be defeated: "I said, 'Look, I'm willing to use my own money to help you fund this guitar'. So they sent some people over to Germany to work with these luthiers who were tension experts. It was quite a process. I believe that each triple neck is worth about fifty thousand dollars - not in materials, but as far as what it costs the company to make them!"

Like Leo Fender in the fifties, Charles Kaman's Ovation company made significant advances in guitar technology during the subsequent two decades. But what made Ovation different from Fender was that they made their name primarily with acoustic, rather than electric guitars. They then went on to pioneer an instrument which successfully bridged the gap between the acoustic and the electric guitar; the electro-acoustic guitar. Kaman did make several forays into the world of the solid-bodied electric with, among others, his odd-shaped Breadwinner instrument, but these were never the successes of the company's stock-in-trade, its electro-acoustics.

The Kaman Corporation began life in 1945 making, not guitars, but helicoptor rotor blades. But Charles Kaman was a fine guitarist with a yen to produce instruments of his own, so Kaman formed

Fusion player Al Di Meola: a long-standing Ovation user

Above: Bon Jovi's Richie Sambora and his $50,000 triple-neck

Below: The parabolic bowl of the Ovation's acoustic body

Ovation in 1967 and, using his knowledge of synthetics gained from life in the aerospace industry, built his first bowl-backed guitar.

Ovation instruments were designed using sound acoustical theories: a parabolic bowl - not unlike that of a radar receiver dish - picks up the vibrations from the guitar's strings and top and focuses them back out through the soundhole.

The acoustical properties of Ovation guitars are well known. The first models, the Standard and Deluxe Balladeers, the Classic and the Josh White, exhibited astonishing clarity and projection. Not only that, but due to the guitars' synthetic construction - the bowl-back is thinner and yet stronger than maple, mahogany or rosewood - they seemed to exhibit consistency of sound from guitar to guitar, giving the lie to the myth that producing good tone was some kind of secret art, only to be handed down through generations.

Kaman's innovations in materials and construction techniques are worthy of great praise in themselves, but history may point to Ovation's combination of the bowl-back theory with the application of piezo transducer technology to produce the first sensibly amplifiable acoustics, as their greatest achievement.

People had experimented with amplifying acoustics before; The Beatles used Gibson's J-

160E with its built-in magnetic pickup, but it didn't sound like a true acoustic; various stick-on 'bug' microphones were starting to find their way on to the market during the early seventies, and the 'Hot Dot', a piezo crystal micro-pickup designed by Barcus Berry Electronics, was also causing something of a stir. But these devices had their limitations: when used with conventional wooden-bodied guitars their tendency to feed back was still a problem. So Ovation buried six piezo transducers, one under each individual bridge saddle of a bowl-back, mated them up to a built-in preamp with volume and tone controls, plugged the instrument in and, lo and behold, it worked!

Ovation's electro-acoustics literally transformed the role of the acoustic guitar in live music - where previously it had been all but unusable on the big stage, due to the associated problems of acoustic boom and howl, now even stadium Rock bands could include acoustic numbers in their live acts. An 'acoustic' guitar could now be plugged in to an amplifier, just like a regular electric guitar or, better still, direct into a large public address system.

American Jazz-Fusion-Classical guitarist Al DiMeola has been using Ovations "...since the beginning, I guess." DiMeola has no reservations about his instrument and its performance: "It's a great guitar. You can get a great level out of it because you've got a direct output."

British singer-songwriter Joan Armatrading

Above: Radical soundholes on this 1992 collector's series

Below: Rock guitarist Lita Ford and her favourite bowl-back

The Who's Peter Townshend with Takamine electro-acoustic

discovered Ovations almost by accident, when she decided on a change of instrument. "I thought the guitar I wanted was a Fender," she recalls, "so I went looking for Fender acoustics but couldn't find one. So then I thought maybe a Gibson, but I couldn't find one of them either."

After trying hordes of different guitars in a London music store the assistant finally showed her an Ovation. "I think he just got fed up with me," jokes Joan. "In the end he said, 'Look, we've got this guitar and all you do is plug it in', and he brought me a Balladeer. It was just the fact that I was able to plug it in really easily that was so impressive at first. But later, once you get over the convenience, you start thinking, well, you're not getting feedback, it projects the sound well and it's a true reproduction of an acoustic sound, which is the most important thing."

While many other manufacturers followed suit with production of their own electro-acoustic guitars - the Japanese companies Takamine, Yamaha,

Washburn and Aria being the most successful - Ovation are still the prime movers in the field of the bowl-back. With the introduction of the Adamas range, which featured distinctive multi-soundholes on the guitar's upper bouts, Kaman took his use of synthetics one stage further. The Adamas' top is made from ultra-thin laminates of carbon graphite, an incredibly strong 'space age' material, and layers of wood. These guitars are said to produce some of the truest and most realistic acoustic tones of any instrument made.

Robert Fripp, late of King Crimson and founder of the 'League of Crafty Guitarists', uses only Ovations, and the final words go to him: "The Ovation is particularly interesting because it's a hybrid instrument - not acoustic, and not electric. Research has shown that ninety percent of a guitar's sound quality comes from the top, and if you're trading off ten percent of the sound for being able to play the thing, then that's a compromise worth making."

Chapter 18

Paul Reed Smith and Eggle

Setting the new standard

In survey after survey, one guitar consistently heads the 'Most Desired Instrument' category: PRS. But who is Paul Reed Smith, where did he come from and what's so special about his guitars?

Paul Reed Smith is a guitarist from Annapolis, Maryland, USA. As a musician Smith had come to the same conclusion as thousands of other guitarists: 'Wouldn't it be great if you could combine the best features of a Fender Stratocaster and a Gibson Les Paul?'

"I had fallen in love with Les Paul Juniors," he admits, "one P90 pickup and they sounded spectacular and played great. I made about one guitar a month for ten years and changed the design, guitar by guitar by guitar, until I came up with something that Fender and Gibson players would both like."

Paul Reed Smith knew that if he wasn't pleasing both markets the guitar would never take off. He also knew that the only way he could put his guitar into serious production was with serious finance. "So I made two prototypes, went on the road, took about three hundred thousand dollars' worth of orders, raised half a million, built a factory and started making them."

PRS guitars are made from the finest tone woods - quilted, flamed and birdseye maple, Honduras

Top of the range Artist model

PRS's 'budget' EG model

mahogany and Brazilian rosewood - and put together without compromise: "We're paying attention to things like neck shape, the way a fingerboard's finished off, the way the edges are, the way the frets are, how level the neck is. I want it to be like old Fenders or Gibsons, so when you look at the neck after thirty years it's still straight."

PRS guitars are stunning to look at, and Smith's cunning pickup switching system, which produces uncanny renditions of both Fender's and Gibson's sounds, make his instruments more than just the perfect hybrid. But although Paul Smith's guitars have been played by many top guitarists, and are the most highly sought after by the 'guitarist in the street', the real star names have eluded him, tending to stick with their Fenders and Gibsons or, like Mark Knopfler, turning to smaller companies like Schecter and Pensa-Suhr. Gary Moore used to be a PRS endorser but gave up playing his because it ran away with him - it was too easy to play!

Still, there are some pretty impressive users of PRS guitars and none more influential than that master of melodic Latin Rock, Carlos Santana.

"I met Paul Reed Smith and he put this guitar into my hand. But he didn't quite have it yet - the lacquer was fine and the finishing was fine but somehow it didn't feel good to me. Then, about three or four years later, he got hold of me and said: 'Hey, Carlos, I want to send you this guitar and if you don't like it then send it back. If you do like it, then call me'. So I picked it up and it sounded like a tenor sax and I thought, 'Wow! I can finally get into those low John Coltrane notes', because all the other guitars sound like an alto. I don't use many gadgets - I just plug in and say 'Sing!' But since I played that guitar I can't go back to anything else - even my original Les Pauls."

Another, fairly recent convert to Paul Reed Smith is Rush's Alex Lifeson, who came to discover PRS after using a variety of guitars throughout the Canadian band's unbelievably successful career. One of these was called a Signature and put together by a friend's company, built around the tried and trusted Fender format, but with a heavier sounding humbucking pickup by the bridge. Unfortunately this project didn't work out, leaving Lifeson on the lookout again. But he'd already tried a PRS and liked it and so he arranged for the company to send a couple up to Toronto: "I took them out of the cases and they were perfect for me," said Alex, "exactly what my friend's Signature guitars always wanted to be." After talking to PRS and arranging one or two slight modifications, such as active single coil pickups, Alex finally settled for PRS Signature models (the company's top-of-the-range instrument, of which only 1000 were made and which was then replaced by the Artist) fitted with humbucking pickups. "It's good to have that sustain and toughness," says Alex, "particularly when we do some of the older material."

Although PRS are known primarily for building guitars with glued-in necks, in the traditional Gibson fashion - unlike Fender-style guitars, which are invariably bolted, or screwed on - Alex Lifeson prefers his PRSes with bolt-on necks. Other modifications include changing the guitar's rotary 5-way pickup selector - which helps utilise various ingenious pickup combinations - for a more standard 3-way toggle switch: "It's something I'm more used to. I wouldn't use the two out-of-phase settings anyway; I'd rather use the amplifier and preamps to change the sound."

We stay with Alex Lifeson for the final endorsement: "PRS guitars are beautiful; they're so well made and so flexible in their sounds."

Eggle

The decision to put Eggle directly after PRS in this way was made to show that, whatever fresh niche is filled by one manufacturer, the gap is never too big to preclude others from jumping in. That this relatively new guitar company is included at all is due to the sheer impact that its instruments have had on the market, in both the UK and Europe. Within the space of a very few years this British manufacturer is being rated among the very best anywhere.

'Mr Tone': Carlos Santana

Uncannily PRS: Eggle's early Climaxe guitar

Patrick Eggle was originally trained at the London College of Furniture to build classical guitars, but decided to start making electric instruments in late 1988. He toyed with a number of designs for a carved top guitar, experimenting with various exotic woods in the process. Receiving a grant from the Prince's Trust he began to build various prototypes and a few production models, trading under the name 'Climaxe'.

Having linked up with businessman/guitarist Andrew Selby, Eggle decided in June '91 to demonstrate his guitars at the International Music Show in London, one month later. The show resulted in orders for over sixty guitars. In August, Selby bought a factory in Coventry and by December the production of Eggle guitars (the Climaxe name having since been abandoned) was in full swing.

The new range of instruments included the Berlin, a mahogany-bodied guitar with a laminated top made from high grade maple.

Amongst the people who began showing an interest in the Berlin was Queen's Brian May: "I've been playing around with one for a while - it's a very nice piece of work. We've been talking about doing a deal together. I don't know whether that will actually happen, because Guild really have the first option, but I was hoping there'd be a way that we could cooperate and Eggle do the British end of it. They're beautifully made, really beautiful."

Another Berlin enthusiast is Midge Ure: "It's great to see British guitars which not only compete with

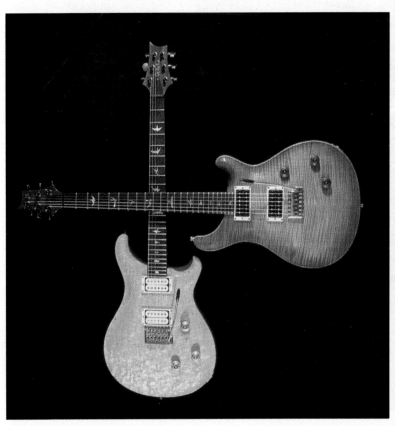

Two PRSes: note the similarity to the Climaxe!

Eggle Berlin and Berlin Pro

the best America can make, but excel!"

During 1992, production increased in line with orders and more staff were taken on at the factory. In July of that year a new range of products was introduced, including the Legend, which was designed in conjunction with British session 'legend' Big Jim Sullivan: "I chose Patrick Eggle to design for me the guitar of my career and he did just that! Quality and performance that I'd only ever dreamed of is now a reality." The Legend features an all maple body with a natural finish, an exquisitely figured top and custom electrics.

Other models then in the range included the Los Angeles, a guitar inspired by Fender's Stratocaster, which has found favour with both Dominic Miller, guitarist with Sting, and John Clark, from Cliff Richard's band.

By mid-1993, eighteen different models were in production, including the new Vienna, the Los Angeles II and the Milan bass. The Coventry factory has since expanded and Patrick now runs a separate facility where he supervises the building of the Eggle acoustic range.

Chapter 19

B.C. Rich

The weird and the wonderful

B.C. Rich Guitars was founded by luthier Bernado Chavez Rico, who began his manufacturing career producing Spanish and classical guitars for the family business, Bernado's Valencian Guitar Shop. Following a commission to restore Bo Diddley's famous rectangular Gretsch, he became interested in building electric guitars.

Although Bernie Rico started by producing copies of Stratocasters and Les Pauls the name of B.C. Rich was soon to become synonymous with

Suzi Quatro's custom-sized Bich bass

Bich guitar

outrageous custom designs for the Rock fraternity. Thus the company soon gained a reputation not only as builders of fine musical instruments, but as producers of fashion statements as well!

B.C. Rich's first production solidbody was the Seagull, produced in 1971 and clearly aimed at the Rock market. The company carried on producing new Rock-orientated models, like the Mockingbird, Bich, Ironbird and Warlock - the latter as seen with Rock guitar goddess Lita Ford on the cover of her album 'Dangerous Curves'. Lita: "I'm used to using my B.C. Rich with the preamp on it. I hardly use anything else. I usually put it straight through 100 watt Marshalls!"

In 1987 the company was divided into several sections and the budget end was purchased by Randy Waltuch. Randy took over the top end of the range the following year and in 1989 bought the remaining interests. Waltuch moved the business to New Jersey where he planned to take the company back to its roots. Randy indicates his dedication and the direction in which he wants B.C. Rich to continue when he states simply: "We've gone back to the basics of woodworking!"

The list of B.C. Rich endorsees continues to grow, the current line-up including such bands as Pantera, Scatterbrain and Skid Row. Rock bad boy, Guns N'Roses' Slash, has three Mockingbirds, and Gene Simmons from Kiss is involved with the company in designing a new bass, 'The Punisher'.

Of course, B.C. Rich has also used British-based endorsees, and probably the best known of these is Detroit-born bass-player/singer Suzi Quatro. Suzi and her band owned a number of B.C. Rich guitars, as her ex-husband and guitarist Len Tuckey recalls: "We had a deal with B.C. Rich for several years and they made us a couple of guitars each. Myself and the other guitarist had Biches and Mockingbirds and Suzi had an Eagle bass and an 8-string Bich. She wanted something lighter so I helped them devise a long scale bass neck on a Bich body and she used that as her main guitar for a number of years."

Chapter 20

Rickenbacker

Individuality, originality and style

Rickenbacker's history goes right back to the early thirties and one of their early instruments, nicknamed the Frying Pan, has a strong claim to the much-disputed title of The World's First Electric Guitar. Ever since then a Rickenbacker has been one of the most individual electric guitars you can buy, and the company is still going strong, producing relatively small quantities of guitars each year and keeping their standards amazingly high.

Although popular in the thirties, forties and fifties - their lap-steel guitars doing especially well - Rickenbacker's ticket to the big time came via The Beatles. John Lennon was the first, buying a short-necked Rickenbacker 325 in 1960 while the group were at near-starvation level playing residencies in Hamburg; George Harrison followed suit three years later with a single-pickup 425. By 1965 The Beatles were the biggest group in the world and representatives of Rickenbacker arranged to meet the young Liverpudlians in New York to present them with more guitars. One of these was still in the experimental stage - the now famous Rickenbacker 12-string.

They met at the hotel. George was laid up with the flu but instantly fell in love with the instrument and started using it at the first opportunity. The guitar, a 360/12 model, was the first Rickenbacker 12-string to have the strings arranged to that as you stroked the pick downwards, you came into contact with the thicker string in each pair first, not the thinner, high-pitched one. This, together with Rickenbacker's unusual construction and pickups, gave the 'jangling' sound that makes the Rickenbacker 12-string sound one of the most easily recognisable in the world.

However, the major exponent of the Rickenbacker 12-string was Roger McGuinn, whose band The Byrds broke new ground in the mid to late sixties by combining Rock with Folk, Jazz and ethnic influences in songs like *Mr. Tambourine Man*, *Turn Turn Turn* and *Eight Miles High*. "I'd been playing an acoustic 12-string with a pickup, but it sounded too fat," McGuinn elaborates, "and then the whole group went to see 'A Hard Day's Night'. George was playing one, so I sold my acoustic and my banjo, bought one and it had a great sound.

Definitive Rick 12-string player: The Byrds' Roger McGuinn

6/12 Twin-neck

Motorhead's Lemmy: father of Thrash Metal?

They've got extremely narrow necks and some people find them hard to play, but I feel very comfortable with them - you just have to re-educate your fingers. I use fingerpicks and a flat pick at the same time, playing banjo-style picking. Rickenbackers make you think in melodies rather than blues scales. You can't bend notes on them very well - you have to play kind of square!"

Around the same time Pete Townshend was using Rickies in a very different manner - thrashing them beyond the point of feedback, and often smashing them to smithereens at the end of the concert. Although he only used the guitars up to 1966, when he changed to using Gibson SGs, one of Rickenbacker's current signature guitars is the Pete Townshend Model. "A couple of guys in the

New 325 short-scale 'John Lennon' Model

them the choice of players as wide-ranging as Paul McCartney (who temporarily ditched his beloved Hofner Violin Bass for one, painted it in psychedelic colours and used it on the later Beatles work), Rush's Geddy Lee, The Who's John Entwistle, Chris Squire, the bass virtuoso with seventies pomp-rockers Yes, and even Lemmy from Motörhead. Actually, Lemmy's choice of bass was more down to fate: "Hawkwind were doing an open-air gig one Summer's day, and the bass player didn't turn up. So they said, 'Who plays bass?' and someone

Above: Early '60s 325, as favoured by Lennon

Below: Byrds-influenced Rick 12-string player, Tom Petty

factory weren't too happy about it," admits Townshend, who has destroyed a fair few Rickenbackers in his time. "They felt it was a jibe, but I don't have romantic misconceptions about musical instruments - they're just wood, after all!"

These three - Harrison, McGuinn and Townshend - showed what Rickenbackers can do. Others, like The Beach Boys, Steppenwolf and Creedence Clearwater Revival followed in their footsteps and today, more than twenty years on, there are more players than ever exploiting that magical sound. Tom Petty, a major McGuinn fan, single-handedly started a new Rickenbacker craze in the mid-seventies by using a solid-bodied 325/12, and even now is strongly identified with the sound. Paul Weller of punk-era mods The Jam, heavily influenced by Townshend, relied upon an assortment of Rickenbacker 330s. Today, hundreds of Indie and sixties-influenced bands base their sound on Rickenbacker guitars.

"I've used my black 360 Rick on every record we've ever done," says Peter Buck of REM. "It's my main guitar; I bought it new, beat it up, splattered blood on it and now it's *my* guitar. You play a guitar for ten years and it's almost part of you."

Johnny Marr used Rickenbackers often in The Smiths' early days. "My 330 is my old faithful," he said, "and I've got a 360 as well, the Roger McGuinn one. They're a really big part of my sound; the 330's got so much power to it, and a really thick bottom end as well as the jangly sound. I ought to get away from them, because when you stick your left hand round a Rickenbacker neck you tend to play in a certain way - well, I do!"

Rickenbacker Model 4001 basses have an almost equally strong following. Their sound is more cutting and piano-like than Fender basses, making

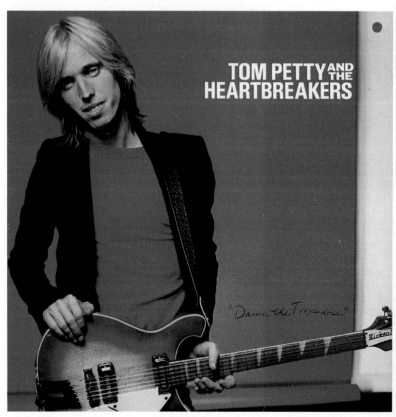

The elegant new Atlantis

Yes's influential bassist Chris Squire

George Harrison and the most famous Rickenbacker of all

pointed at me. They hung a Rickenbacker around my neck and said, 'Off you go!'"

And what's the reason for Rickenbacker's continuing popularity? "I think we've come full circle," says John Hall, Rickenbacker's President. "We've been hearing the same sounds for so long that guitarists are looking for something different, and a great number find it with our instruments. Rickenbackers are a kind of radical tradition!"

If your favourite guitarist plays a Rickenbacker, there's only one way to get the same sound - get a Rickenbacker yourself. You'll never regret it.

Chapter 21

Steinberger and Status

New materials to solve old problems

"Definitely *the* bass for the eighties," was Police guitarist Andy Summers' reaction to Sting's newly acquired Steinberger bass, in early 1982.

Several attempts had been made, throughout the preceding seventies especially, to offer something unique and 'different' to guitarists and bass players, whether in materials or by way of construction. These efforts, including aluminium necks from Kramer and Travis Bean, sliding pickups from Dan Armstrong and Gibson, various see-through plastic guitars and one or two 'foldaway' instruments, were met with varying degrees of indifference. But none could have hoped to match the impact created by the radical concept of Ned Steinberger in combining the use of space age materials with a minimalist design ethic to produce the first of his series of distinctive instruments.

Colloquially referred to as 'plastic' or 'stick' basses and guitars, due to their material composition and slim, 'headless' appearance, Steinberger instruments caused many a stir within the infamously conservative world of the bassist and guitar player.

Ned Steinberger was a freelance industrial designer who gained much of his musical instrument knowledge and experience whilst working for American bass luthier Stuart Spector. For his own guitars Ned disregarded accepted conventions in an attempt to address many of the inherent problems associated with the bass guitar - e.g. tuning, balance, sustain, comfort, etc.

Convention dictated that a bass's tuning machines were located on a necessarily large headstock, which would then be offset by a correspondingly large body, making the bass guitar a physically daunting prospect. Steinberger had the inspired idea of relocating the tuners on to the body of his bass, thus negating the need for a headstock and allowing for considerable reductions in body size. With string tension applied over a physically shorter length, general stability should be improved too.

The idea seemed good, so Steinberger built a wooden prototype, finding that it possessed excellent balance and comfort characteristics - but sounded awful! The problem was the wood. Wood

Tin Machine's Reeves Gabrels and his Steinberger guitar

tends to absorb vibrations and creates 'dead spots' at certain points on the neck, where notes sound dull and muted and sustain is inhibited. Conventionally compensated for by making the instrument larger - i.e. increasing its mass - Steinberger's little wooden bass could only result in poor performance.

So alternative materials were sought which were stronger and more rigid than wood. As with Charles Kaman's Ovation guitars the aerospace industry provided the answer, its classic requirement of minimal mass with phenomenal strength having resulted in the development of many advanced plastics. Steinberger built a second, more successful prototype

Allan Holdsworth and Steinberger 'stick' guitar

from these materials. After intensive experimentation to find the most suitable combination of plastics, the headless Steinberger 'stick' bass was launched to great acclaim.

Bass-playing and singing frontmen, such as Geddy Lee of Rush and Sting of The Police, found the freedom from the bulk and weight of conventional basses very creative. Sting: "It takes the weight off my spine and makes it easier for me to sing, plus I can move around much more easily on stage."

Steinberger went on to apply his revolutionary principles to guitars, meeting with similar success. Guitarists in all musical areas have made use of them, from David Bowie, who plays a distinctive chromed version, to Mike Rutherford of Genesis and Mike and the Mechanics, and to that enigmatic

Steinberger 'headed' guitar, the elegant Sceptre

master of the guitar, Allan Holdsworth.

Rutherford actually helped Steinberger design a 'bodied' version of his guitar: "I used one of the original 'stick' Steinbergers," explains Mike, "and looked pretty ridiculous with it, because of my height and its lack of any dimensions. So I asked Steinberger if they would change the design for me to something bigger, and they refused, because they're a small company and couldn't afford to get into the business of making one-offs."

So one night Mike laid his guitar on top of a piece of card, drew a shape around it which seemed to work, commissioned luthier Roger Giffin to build one and promptly began to use the instrument on stage. Steinberger later saw it, asked if they could have a look at it and ended up using the instrument as the basis for a new production model. "I had a feeling when they saw it that they'd like it," adds Rutherford, with some degree of satisfaction.

Allan Holdsworth's use of Steinbergers extends to the cleverly designed TransTrem, which moves all six strings uniformly up or down. On regular tremolo systems the bass strings detune more readily than the treble, so where the thinner, top E might detune only marginally, the same downward pressure on the arm could drop the bottom strings' pitch by four or five times as much. The TransTrem can also be locked into different keys, in semi-tone steps over a limited range, allowing the guitarist to change key at will.

"I stopped using the whammy bar in the normal sense - like down," says Holdsworth. "I only use it to take things up, which is what I like about the

Status 5-string: materials conventional and modern

Steinberger. All the strings change uniformly, so if I want to bend up a tone on the D string, I know that if I move the arm the same amount for a note on the G string, I'll still get a tone. It's a great machine, although it took me a long time to get used to it."

Status

One company which rose to prominence making bass guitars which sported a novel combination of hi-tech materials, exotic woods and advanced electronics was Status Graphite, the creation of a young English luthier called Rob Green.

These impressive basses embodied many of the characteristics desired by the ever-growing school of serious and/or professional players emerging during the early eighties.

The arrival of these fashionably headless basses coincided with the search to find an instrument which suited the funky and increasingly popular 'slapping' style, as personified by occasional Status user Mark King.

Initially utilising the headless design pioneered by Steinberger and a neck-through-body construction, Status used woven carbon fibre and resin composites in order to produce an inherently strong yet not unduly heavy bass. The man-made 'phenolic' fingerboard was harder than even ebony, and induced a bright, clear, ringing sustain.

Rob Green's examples proved successful from the outset, winning

Note the carbon fibre weave on the necks of these Statuses

favour with many top players. Status also benefitted in no small way from the ground-breaking advances made only a couple of years earlier by Steinberger's radical 'stick' bass. As with the Steinberger, the headless instrument's tuners were located in the 'tail' of the bass and required the use of special strings with an attachment ball at both ends.

The quality of build and standard of facilities offered by Status has always been very high. Incorporation of a variety of attractive woods in the bodies helps lend these high-technology instruments a traditional look, which all bassists can relate to. Initial association with one particular musical style has widened as the basses' powerful sound and wide-ranging capability has become more generally accepted.

A convert to Status Graphite is session bass player Tony Levin, who has taken possession of a top-of-the-line Empathy Matrix, insisting that this one bass allows him the freedom to move from the percussive sounds chosen when playing on Peter Gabriel's albums, to the smooth and mellow bass tones required on tracks by, say, Joan Armatrading.

John 'Rhino' Edwards, Status Quo's fine bassist, is a confirmed Status fan, arguing that they are the only instruments he has tried which stand up to the rigours of constant use with a hard-working Rock band. Insists Rhino: "I've been trying out loads of guitars but the only one I still really rave about is the Status."

Chapter 22

The Vintage phenomenon

Moncy for nothing or investment in musical history?

In the mid to late sixties, something rather curious began to happen in guitar playing circles: certain influential musicians were reported hunting out the older American electric guitars; especially Fenders and Gibsons and most especially those built during the fifties and very early sixties.

These older guitars - so players like Eric Clapton, Pete Townshend, Tony Hicks, Alvin Lee and Steve Marriott would have us believe - played better and sounded superior to their modern counterparts. It seemed that the demand placed on the guitar

The seriously sought-after 1958 Gibson Flying Vee

Right: Fender Strats from the first year of production onwards

factories by the aspiring Harrisons and Hendrixes of the day had simply been too great, forcing quantity up and quality down. But could any business refuse the chance to turn in a fast buck on the back of what was surely just a blip, a temporary abberation in the popularity of the guitar? Of course it couldn't. So production roared ahead while quality control took a back seat. As an example of this, Gibson's serial numbers shot from 000001 to 999999 twice, during a short period in the mid-sixties, creating confusion as regards dating guitars and showing clearly just how many instruments were being built.

But there's more to it than simple numbers. When companies like Gibson and Fender made their original Les Pauls and Stratocasters, they were largely unaware of the importance of, for instance, the coil-wire or the magnets used in the construction of their pickups. Fender probably didn't think it mattered whether a Strat was finished in cellulose lacquer or modern polyester; and Gibson were doubtless unaware that their original neck dimensions had been perfect,

whereas the narrower necks perceived by the new designers as preferable, were in fact less player-friendly!

So, small changes in production methods and component buying - changes which seemed

Gary Moore's Les Pauls: '57, a '58 and two '59s

inconsequential at the time - conspired to create a substantial shift from the initial design brief.

A case in point is the humbucking pickup. Originally this unit was designed by Gibson's Seth Lover using alnico magnets (alnico is an acronym for **al**uminium, **ni**ckel and **co**balt) and shellac-coated copper windings of a given gauge. Now, pickups don't have to use expensive alnico, or natural-coated wire, but when such specifications are altered - in this case for reasons of ecomomy - so is the pickup's tone character. And the better players could hear the difference.

With Fender, the pundits could point at an actual date when it all fell apart: that fateful day in 1965 when Leo Fender sold out to CBS for $13,000,000! Of course, really it didn't all go downhill overnight, even though having a multi-national corporation at the helm inevitably led to some accountancy-based decisions! The simple fact was that the buyout coincided with the public's desire for more instruments and the quality problems associated with that.

Almost all old guitars have some sort of premium attached to their value today, but there are several real vintage stars. These are the classics: those instruments which sounded best and proved to be the most usable on stage and the most musical in the studio.

Gibson's Les Paul Standard of '57 to '60 is the archetypal vintage electric guitar. This is the one that really started it all, when guitarists like Mike Bloomfield began using it in America, and Eric Clapton, Jimmy Page and Peter Green emulated him in Great Britain. It's probably no exaggeration to say that those guitarists and that guitar created the Rock guitar sound that we know today - distorted and aggressive, but simultaneously smooth and sustaining. In the late sixties, original Les Pauls - of which only 1,700 or so were made - began fetching £400 or more in London guitar stores, at a time when a brand new Telecaster could be bought for less than half that!

Other Gibson guitars were soon to attract Rock and Blues players' attention. Due to the use of very similar pickups and electrics, supremely playable necks and a good, worn-in feel, ES335s from 1958 to the early sixties were soon snapped up, as were the buffalo-horned SGs of 1960 onwards. Eric Clapton regularly used both these instruments with Cream and so accelerated their status to that of musical icons.

Fender's original Stratocaster and Telecaster models, those from the first days of production up until the mid sixties, also began gaining ground. Strats and Teles were searched out by musicians, collections started to be assembled and the considerable industry which exists today in old guitars - and old amplifiers, effects pedals and anything associated with the music of the time -

Above: A stunning example of an early Gretsch 6120

Below: '50s Fenders: a one-pickup Esquire and a two-pickup Tele

began to take shape. Today, the most collectable Fenders are generally examples from the fifties. But Fender's Custom colours - metallics in particular - from right up to the end of the sixties are also much sought after.

It's worth reiterating that the guitars which first become collectable did so because they were the most usable. This is why basic Gibson and Fender models were so highly prized. These are among the most player friendly of any electric guitars, with sensible control layouts and pickup switching. Other manufacturers - notably Gretsch and to a lesser extent Rickenbacker in America, and almost all British and European manufacturers - tended to incorporate unnecessary complications and so features which looked great in the catalogues were often obstacles to the guitarist's creativity.

In fact, Gretsches were so frowned upon by the burgeoning Rock and Blues fraternity that business in Gretsch guitars all but dried up during the seventies. Then, when young bands of the subsequent decade began looking for something cool in appearance - recreating the Mod look of sixties Pop - they adopted these guitars, which not only could be bought cheaply but fitted the bill perfectly. Naturally it wasn't long before the public saw Gretsch guitars in the hands of bands like Haircut 100, Spear Of Destiny, The Cult, The Eurythmics etc., and the prices of these instruments soared. A similar phenomenon can be witnessed in the nineties, as Indie band after Indie band take up Fender's once discarded Jaguar and Jazzmaster models.

While other manufacturers might discount Gibson's and Fender's supremecy in the vintage market, possibly holding up models of their own as evidence, there's no denying the fact that the vast majority of guitars designed today owe the most to these two innovators. And this is directly due to the musicians showing the manufacturers what they wanted; by turning their noses up at the new and deliberately seeking out the old.

Today, almost any old guitar has some vintage value, even though as a musical tool it might leave much to be desired.

But probably the most bizarre part of the whole vintage issue is that the very instruments which created the desire to find original, unadulterated guitars - those poorer quality, mass produced Gibsons and Fenders of the late sixties and early seventies - are themselves now attracting vintage value. As they say, there's nowt so strange as folks!

A fabulous 'dot-neck' Gibson ES335 from 1958

Chapter 23

Warwick basses

Streamlined German success story

Although Warwick basses were launched as recently as 1982, the manufacture of musical instruments is something that runs in Hans-Peter Wilfer's family; his father Fred ran the legendary German guitar company Framus.

The popular Warwick Streamer bass

Respected and influential bassist Jack Bruce

Similarly based in Germany, Warwick soon became known for high standards of quality and playability, and recognised for their natural finishes, where oil and wax is rubbed into the wood for protection and preservation. Warwick basses are graceful and curvacious and extremely slim and modern in appearance. This, allied to their use of exotic timbers such as wenge and bubinga, the fitting of industry standard hardware and well researched pickups and active electronics, ensured that Warwick quickly found a niche among the most desirable instruments available.

"I play a lot of different basses," comments bass virtuoso Doug Wimbish, who has played with many great artists, including Jeff Beck and Mick Jagger. Wimbish also has his own funk/rap/techno band

Foreigner's Ricky Wills and his Streamer

The Who's John Entwistle designed this Buzzard bass

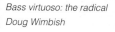

*Bass virtuoso: the radical
Doug Wimbish*

Tackhead and in 1993 joined the American black rock group Living Colour. "Right now I'm using Warwicks," continues Doug; "all instruments have inherent character and I'm getting on with the Warwicks more and more."

Wimbish's bass playing is akin to that of Jimi Hendrix's guitar style, with his outrageous use of string-bending and general guitar contortions, plus the utilisation of fuzz-boxes, echo units and even samplers to create his wild sounds.

The Who's bassist John Entwistle had Warwick make him his distinctive Buzzard bass. This outlandish instrument filled Entwistle's updated requirement for an instrument based loosely on a Gibson Explorer body, but fitted with a neck which felt like an old Fender Precision.

To complement Jack Bruce's individual jazz-based style, Cream's ex-bassist has used a Warwick fretless for some years now. "The reason I'm playing a Warwick," states Jack, emphatically, "is because it's the best instrument at the moment for me."

Chapter 24

Washburn

Traditional and modern, from Chicago to Korea

Alongside Yamaha and Ibanez, the modern Washburn company has built an excellent name for itself making a whole range of guitars, from acoustics through to Rock-orientated electrics and basses. Beware, though, because the Washburns that are sometimes referred to in the same breath as Martins by vintage guitar buffs are not the same guitars that we buy today; the real, early

Washburn's attractive EA series electro-acoustic, in white

The EA40 12-string in natural finish

Washburns were made in Chicago from 1876 through to 1929 and the name of Washburn was acquired by the present owners in the 1970s.

Nowadays, Washburn designs its guitars in the USA and then has them made by factories in Chicago (where they produce high quality instruments in small numbers), Japan and Korea, a policy which lets them offer a guitar to suit just about every pocket and playing style. Many of Washburn's seventies and early eighties electrics had a strong Gibson influence, but they've taken care to develop a style of their own, in particular

their most widely-used 'Festival' acoustic-electric series. These are good-looking acoustic guitars with cutaways and built-in pickups: Bob Dylan has one, as does George Harrison, Bono from U2 and Extreme's Nuno Bettencourt.

Washburn realise as well as any other manufacturer that it's the personal touch that sells guitars, and their biggest scoop of late has been to

Above: Washburn's prime endorser, Extreme's Nuno Bettencourt with his N4

Below: Washburn's Steve Stevens model

build a solid electric model for Extreme's extremely able young guitarist, Nuno Bettencourt, who actually uses his all the time - unlike many other 'endorsers' of major guitar companies. "I can't play anything else right now," exclaims Nuno. "It literally just plays - it plays with you and doesn't fight back. And although it's got a neck that's bolted on to the body, it's also got this great cutaway design that means there's no heel to get in the way when you're playing up the top of the neck.

"I also got rid of the tone control, because no-one uses one anyway, and we moved the pickup switch so that it's easy to hit without fumbling around. The pickups on my own guitar are a Bill Lawrence LX500 humbucker by the bridge and a Gibson pickup by the neck. They'll be making a full, handmade version and there'll be a half-price model too, which is more of a production thing. That one won't have all the features of the expensive one, but it *will* have the really funky headstock that I drew up!"

Other names on Washburn's user list include such luminaries as The Edge, Bob Geldof, Dave Gilmour, Joni Mitchell, Jimmy Page and Pete Townshend. Like Bettencourt, most of these artists are regularly seen with their instruments, a testimony not only to Washburn's Artist Relations programme, but to their eminently playable guitars as well.

The cheaper Bettencourt model, the N2

Chapter 25

Yamaha

The company who made Japanese guitars respectable and credible

Billy Sheehan, Mr Big's virtuoso bassist chooses Yamaha

Although this company has been in the business of making musical instruments since as far back as 1887, most guitarists will first have become aware of Yamaha during the sixties and seventies, when their low-priced but high-quality acoustic guitars, like the FG-140, were all the rage. But times move on, and today Yamaha is one of the biggest music

corporations in the world, their instruments being played by some of the most respected musicians in all styles.

The first 'original' Japanese electric guitar to gain a worldwide reputation (the Japanese were notorious for their copies) was Yamaha's SG-2000. This success was due in no small part to the stature

The MSG/Image: Yamaha's English-designed traditional electric

of one particular guitarist who adopted it - Carlos Santana.

During the seventies Santana had a massive reputation as a melodic player with a beautiful sustaining sound and an intellectual approach to his music and equipment which lent huge influence to any instrument he played. Carlos had always been a dedicated Gibson user, being associated mainly with Les Pauls and SGs, and he single-handedly lifted the profile of the company's unpopular L6S of the mid seventies: "That was why I left Gibson altogether," explains Carlos. "I was using that guitar and managing to get certain tones out of it, but when I went to Japan and Yamaha offered me this other one, Gibson got really uptight and they said, 'We've got these new pickups' and this and that. So they put in my hands this new Les Paul and it sounded like somebody with a bad cold - real nasal problems. And the guy got really insulting and said, 'You're only going to use this Japanese stuff because they give you guitars.' I said, 'I beg your pardon?' and I broke my relationship with them right there and then."

Yamaha's SG continued its success through that decade and a whole range was built up around its styling, from the lowliest SG-200 to the top-of-the-range SG-3000S. But by the early eighties the electric guitar was in trouble; synthesiser bands had taken over from Punk, which had itself poured scorn on what it saw as the musical dodos of the previous generation, including the likes of Santana. And when the guitar's popularity returned, halfway through the decade, instruments like the Les Paul and Yamaha's SG were out of fashion, replaced by tremolo-laden, so-called 'Superstrats' from Kramer, Charvel and almost everyone else.

Although Yamaha have tried to replace the SG - and indeed have continued to make them in limited numbers - their concentration on emulation rather than innovation in solid body guitar design has meant no real success to date. The closest they came was with a design from British employee Martyn Booth, whose guitar was basically a small-bodied solid 335-style instrument, built using Paul Reed Smith's ethic of classical styling and functional design. Although Booth's MSG/Image was a hit with such influential guitarists as the late Alan Murphy of Go West and Level 42, Yamaha never really got behind the guitar, preferring to stick with American designs which were more derivative of Fenders and Jacksons, etc.

One of the finest Jazz players: Martin Taylor and his AE Yamaha

In the field of the bass guitar, however, Yamaha have had impressive successes. Paul McCartney was a regular Yamaha user, and such respected bassists as Nathan East (Eric Clapton) and Leland Sklar (James Taylor and Phil Collins) have recently taken up Yamaha instruments. Nathan East went to the factory in Japan and sat down with them to design a 5-string bass. It took a while to arrive but when it did Nathan was most impressed. "From the moment I took it out of the case it felt comfortable," he said.

Leland Sklar has been James Taylor's bassist since the days of 'Sweet Baby James'. A melodic and adventurous player his style is characterised by a round woody tone and a smooth legato style which stems, in part, from the fact that Leland fits thin mandolin fretwire to his basses, so that sliding lightly up the neck produces a pseudo 'fretless' sound. Listen to James Taylor's version of Carole King's *You've Got a Friend* to hear the definitive Sklar.

Leland's main instrument over the years has been an ancient Fender Precision, signed by the many artists with whom he has worked. But his longtime association with the people at Yamaha USA has now born fruit. Sklar had referred to Yamaha's

Bill Nelson's playing with '70s band Bebop Deluxe was highly advanced. Here he is with his Yamaha 3000S

Bass playing sessioneer Nathan East

Yamaha's electro-acoustic APX guitar

previous basses as "not players' instruments; more like something you'd hang on a wall," but as he embarked on Phil Collins' 1990 World Tour he was really enthusiastic: "I've got a 4-string and a 5-string and they're making me a fretless 4-string which should be ready when I get back."

Along with Ovation, Aria, Washburn and Takamine, Yamaha have been at the forefront of electro-acoustic technology, and their APX range is rated as among the best in the world. But less well appreciated is the fact that the company produces traditional, and not-so-traditional, jazz guitars. Martin Taylor is one of the world's foremost jazzers and a Yamaha player almost exclusively.

"I'm using an AE1200 which I'm very happy with. Also, I've designed a guitar with Martyn Booth; it's an archtop, and you'll also be able to bring an acoustic sound in, because it has an acoustic bridge pickup in it as well."

Yamaha guitars and basses are rated almost as highly as any instruments made today. The company must be applauded for raising the quality of Far Eastern guitar production to the point where their Taiwanese guitars and basses are built as well as the best American and European instruments. And if they use their resources to continue the quest for the individual, rather than following the trends of fashion, Yamaha will be a force to be reckoned with for another hundred years.

Chapter 26

Zemaitis

Bespoke guitar maker to Rock's aristocracy

Hand built by British luthier Tony Zemaitis, these rather exclusive instruments carry a particularly high price tag. Probably the single best-known user of Zemaitis guitars is Rolling Stones guitarist Ron Wood who, during his time in The Faces, employed a trio of Zemaitis metal-fronted instruments. Ron

Zemaitis has his own recollections of that first meeting with Ron Wood: "The first time that Woody came here he had Ronnie Laine with him, and I honestly believed I was being set up for Candid Camera. They were like the original Two Ronnies, those two. They were pointing at the guitars on the wall, cracking jokes, saying, 'I'll have that! And that. Can you make me one of these?' I really thought they were winding me up, but then the dollars hit the table and I realised they meant it! And Ronnie didn't just want one guitar, he bought twelve or thirteen altogether - one for Keith, one for Mick, and so on."

Ron's Zemaitis electrics were all in Tony's vaguely Les Paul shape, although Tony has always made other styles. Eric Clapton's 'Big Bertha' 6-string acoustic was one

This pearl-fronted Zemaitis is a visual stunner!

Distinctive headstock with engraved name and trussrod plates

recalls: "There was the silver plated one; the black one with the round silver 'thing' that I used on songs like *Stay With Me*, and the mother of pearl one. I had the silver one knocked off in the early seventies and Tony Zemaitis made me one very similar. But he made it a policy never to make two the same and that second one was never quite up to the first one; I still have it though."

Engraved metal fronts are distinctive Zemaitis trademarks

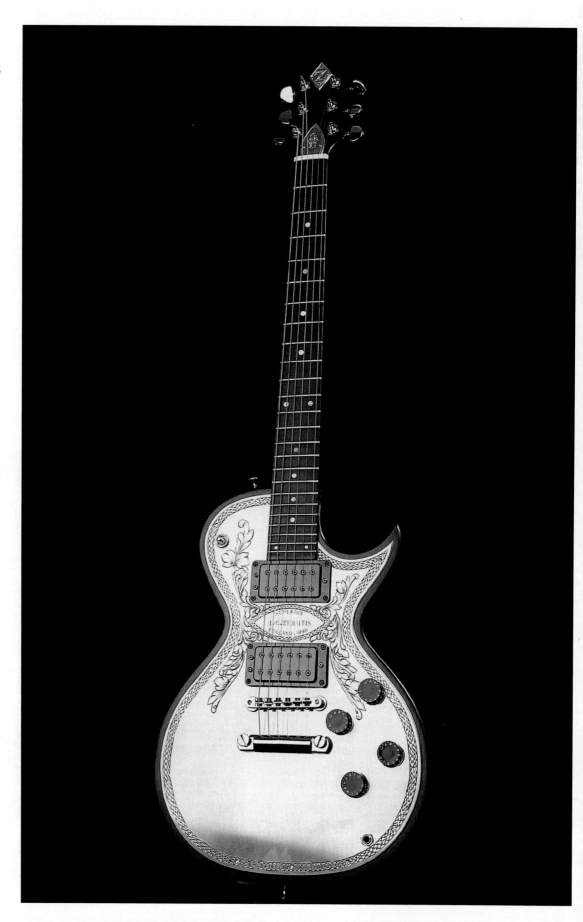

An unusual group of rare Zemaitis electrics and acoustics

of them. Like many of Zemaitis' acoustic instruments Big Bertha produced amazing sustain from a heart-shaped soundhole - a feature which Tony also used on the acoustic bass he built for Pink Floyd's guitarist David Gilmour in 1978.

"Clapton's 'Ivan The Terrible' 12-string was a bit of a special one," explains Tony, talking of sustain. "He and Rory Gallagher once took it to the Gibson factory to have it tested and the bridge on that guitar turned out to give a thirty second sustain, and eighteen seconds was the best they could get out of a Gibson acoustic. We later put some silver edging on that guitar to make it prettier and the sustain dropped to twenty-six seconds, which is splitting hairs, I know, but twenty-six seconds still wasn't bad."

The Black Crowes' Rich Robinson is a recent Zemaitis acquisitor. Having been influenced by The Faces and Stones it's not surprising that Rich should want to emulate his early heroes. He also happens to think Tony's guitars are very special: "I'm kind of partial to Teles," says Rich, "so I talked him into making a Tele version. It took three and a half months and I was wondering about it the whole

time and I thought, 'Man, it's either going to be so good that I'm never going to want to play another guitar, or it's going to suck!'" Fortunately the guitar was everything Rich expected of it: "You'd be hard pressed to find someone who takes as much time and care with a musical instrument as Tony Zemaitis," he exclaims. "Even if I never played it again I would put the guitar on display in my house, because it's a fine work of art."

Of course, exclusivity doesn't come cheap and in the case of Zemaitis guitars people generally talk in thousands, not hundreds of pounds. But while Tony is more than happy to build guitars for the average musician, his list of clientele does, however, read like a Who's Who of Rock. "I remember a friend of ours had an Australian girlfriend," laughs Tony, "and he brought her round for a visit one day. He'd told her about the famous musicians that used to call in and I think she thought he was trying it on. But the day they arrived they came into the kitchen and Eric Clapton was sitting at the table, with George Harrison standing at the other side. We practically had to pick her up off the floor!"